REALIZE AND REJOICE!

A Study of
the Lenten Epistles

Series A

Richard Carl Hoefler

REALIZE AND REJOICE!

Scripture quotations are from the *Revised Standard Version* except where otherwise indicated.

ISBN 0-89536-468-9

PRINTED IN U.S.A.

DEDICATED TO

ST. JOHN'S LUTHERAN CHURCH

SPRINGFIELD, OHIO

Table of Contents

ACKNOWLEDGMENTS

Appreciation is expressed to the Rev. Dr. J. Benjamin Bedenbaugh, Professor of New Testament, Lutheran Theological Southern Seminary, Columbia, South Carolina, who read this manuscript and offered suggested changes and corrections. This acknowledgement does not mean that all the interpretations of biblical passages expressed in this book meet with Dr. Bedenbaugh's approval. Many of the friendly discussions of conflicting interpretations were not brought to mutual agreement. However, the stimulation of such conversations was vital to the completion of this work.

Jesus Christ Superscar

Ash Wednesday

2 Corinthians 5:20b-6:2

Lent is a period when we take a special look at the cross — not an empty cross, but one bearing upon it the body of our Lord. The message is clear. It is not the cross that saves us, no matter how "old" and "rugged"; rather our salvation rests solely upon the one who hangs nailed to the cross. It is the suffering and death of Christ that saves. The wounds on his body are the signs of our redemption.

There is a second message that makes up the theme of Lent. As he died for us, so we are to *live* for him. As he offered his body a dying sacrifice to us, so we are to offer our bodies a living sacrifice to him.

In the Second Lesson for Ash Wednesday, 2 Corinthians 5:20b-6:2, Paul develops this second message of Lent and brings together "Christ's death for us" and "our life in him." This text appears in a section of Paul's letter to the Corinthians dealing with what it means to "live in Christ." He describes this life as being an ambassador for Christ.

The Greek word Paul uses here is *presebeuein*, translated "ambassador." Originally it had two meanings. First, it referred to a representative of the emperor who was sent to imperial provinces with a direct commission to speak on the emperor's behalf and act in his stead.

This would indicate that Paul was pointing out that we are directly commissioned by God to represent him and his work in the world.

The second meaning of *persebeuein* (ambassador) is even more suggestive. When a country had waged war against Rome and was defeated, the Roman senate met to decide the fate of the conquered country. If the senate decided to make it a province of Rome, ten ambassadors were sent along with the victorious generals to determine the terms of peace, establish boundaries, and draw up a constitution. Thus ambassadors were men charged with the responsibility of bringing vanquished people into the family of the Roman Empire. This means that when Paul calls us to be ambassadors of Christ we are commissioned to be peacemakers. We are envoys of the gospel of peace. We are sent forth to proclaim and establish a relationship of reconciliation between God and his people — to actually invite and bring people into the family of God.

Word of Warfare

The first thing Paul says is "be reconciled to God" (5:20b). Originally the word "reconciliation" was not a religious term but a word of warfare. It was a word used to describe the establishment of peace between two warring parties, thereby bringing them together in a relationship of harmony.

The direction of this action is important. We are reconciled *to God*. The process of salvation begins with God. He is not angry but so loved the world that he sent his son to seek and restore those who make war against him. God does not dig the gulf or erect the barrier between himself and us. We are the bullheaded bulldozers of the gulf; we are the barrier-builders. God is not estranged from us; we are estranged from him.

The tragedy of our rebellion is that we can break the relationship between ourselves and God, but we cannot rebuild it. When Cortez invaded Central America with his Spanish conquistadors, he burned all the ships which had brought him to the new land so that there could be no turning back. As sinners, we likewise are so determined in our escape from God that we burn our bridges behind us, and there is no turning back. If a bridge is to be built, it must begin on God's side.

The message of reconciliation that Paul proclaims is that God has acted. He has taken the decisive step to reunite himself with his rebellious creation. Calvary is that point in history where God builds his bridge. He places a cross in the gulf of separation between himself and us. On that crossbridge he places the innocent body of his son, crucified!

During the First World War an officer in the Corps of Engineers went out to repair a broken communications line. When he arrived at the spot of the severed wire, he climbed a tree to splice the dangling lines. Suddenly a bomb exploded beneath him, riddling his body with shrapnel. He knew that he did not have strength enough to repair the line, so with a last desperate effort he reached out and grabbed one end of the line and with the other hand caught hold of the remaining line. His body became a human conductor and the current flowed.

On Calvary, with his hands stretched forth on the cross, our Lord held the hand of God and with the other hand he reached out and grabbed hold of us. The gulf was bridged, the barrier was eliminated, and Christ became the divine-human conductor. The powerful current of God's grace flowed!

Something Done, Something Undone

It is not enough to know that God is forgiving love. We are not saved by education or knowledge. Nor is it enough to recognize our need to love God and seek his forgiveness. We are not saved by a willing decision to choose God. Christ crucified on the cross is not a sign revealing God's love to the ignorant; nor is it a magnet drawing forth a response from the indifferent. Rather it is a *deed* determined, dared and done by God. If we are to be saved, something must be done and something must be undone. The gulf, the barrier between God and us, must be destroyed and a bridge built in the void, and that bridge must be crossed! Paul states that in order for this two-fold action to be accomplished Christ must become *sin*.

With the words, "he made him to be sin" (5:21), Paul presents the gospel of the crucifixion in all its mystery and wonder. For us, this phrase, "made sin," is one of the most profound and decisive statements in all of the New Testament. This phrase strikes the tone of the whole Lenten Season and presents the basis for the new bridge-relationship between us and our God.

Note! Paul says, "He made him to be sin." He does not say, "made him a sinner." Christ is without sin. Christ knew no sin. The phrase, "made him to be sin," means treated the innocent one as responsible for sin, and therefore made him bear in his innocence the consequences of all sin — endure the death which is the destiny of sin. Only as Christ is blameless and without guilt can he take upon himself our guilt and suffer our punishment.

A man once owed a debt of ten thousand dollars. He sat down to figure out how he could pay it back. His salary with all possible overtime would be about one thousand dollars a month. Conceivably he could pay back the debt in ten months. But here's the catch; the man's living expenses were over a thousand dollars a month. So even though he worked as hard as he could, his expenses ate up his earnings, and he had nothing left at the end of the month to eliminate the debt. The sad truth is that he only became deeper in debt.

So with us. The best we can do merely meets the demands of

living. We have nothing left over to pay against the debts our sins have accumulated. We are helpless. All of our efforts are in vain. If we are to be free from debt, someone must assume the payments for us. This Christ does.

Granted this analogy is far too commercial to be a direct analogy of what Christ does for us. God is no Shylock demanding his pound of flesh; Christ's death is not blood-money paid to a gangster-like God. But the note of total helplessness to solve the demanding problem is a valid analogy. In addition, the story points out the true nature of our dilemma. The tragedy of the man in our story is not his refusal or unwillingness to pay off the debt, but the total impossibility of doing so. He was willing to do anything, work as hard as he could, as long as he could, but still it would not solve his problem.

So with us. It is not our unwillingness or our refusal to return to God that is our tragic state, but our total helplessness. Our best is simply not enough.

A few years ago the young people in California had a fad called, "Jumping to Catalina." They would run and leap from the cliff in the direction of Catalina Island. Twenty feet was considered a good jump. Some jumped as far as twenty-five feet. But as great as their efforts might sound, their futility was evident. Catalina Island was thirty-two miles away. So our efforts to bridge the gap between ourselves and our God are but fad-like efforts of futility. We can jump but a few feet when a broad jump of miles is required.

Therefore, the cross is not an exhibition that all is well, but proof positive that nothing is well. We are helpless before the requirements of God's holiness and justice. God is just as well as loving, and therein lies the cause of our helplessness. God's justice must be met, as well as his grace and mercy given.

The death of Christ on the cross brings together the justice and the love of God. It is a deed which deals with both justice and love at the same time. It is a deed done to change the relationship between God and us. This is the keystone of the entire act of redemption. Christ does not just *show* us the truth of God's love, or attempt to *convince* us of God's love, but he *changes* the relationship between us and God so that God's justice might be satisfied and his love experienced.

During the Revolutionary War there was a preacher named Peter Miller. He lived near a person who hated him intensely. One day Miller's neighbor was found guilty of treason and was sentenced to death. Hearing about this, Pastor Miller walked sixty miles to George Washington's headquarters and interceded on behalf of his neighbor.

General Washington listened to Pastor Miller's plea, but told him that there was no new basis for pardoning his friend. "Your friend is guilty and I know of nothing new that changes the situation," said Washington.

"My friend?" Pastor Miller came back. "He is not my friend. Far from it! In fact, he considers me to be his worst enemy!" Washington was astounded and replied, "You mean you walked sixty miles to save the life of a man who calls you enemy? That puts the whole matter in a different light. Because of what *you* have done, I will grant the request for *your* sake." The man was pardoned.

General Washington found in the guilty man no basis to change his verdict, but he did find in Pastor Miller's effort a basis for pardon. So God finds no basis in us to establish a new relationship with us. In Christ's deed, however, God does have a basis to declare us pardoned. God sees Christ's righteousness and declares us to be righteous.

The righteousness of Christ becomes the object of God's judgment of our sins. Therefore, "in him" we are judged and found innocent. It is on Christ that the full force of God's justice and judgment falls. At the same time "in Christ" we find shelter from guilt. Two things happen in the action of Christ's death on the cross — our sins are transferred to him and his righteousness is transferred to us, "so that in him we might become the righteousness of God" (5:21b). Something is done and something is undone.

The Mask of Righteousness

On Halloween our children celebrate by covering their innocent faces with ugly masks. The more frightening the mask the better. In the process of redemption this Halloween custom is reversed, the mask of Christ's righteousness covers the ugliness of our sinful appearance. God looks at us and sees not what we are, but what we appear to be wearing — the mask of Christ's righteousness. And God declares us to be righteous.

Working with God

In Paul's previous letter to the Corinthians he announced that "we are God's fellow-workers" (1 Corinthians 3:9). Here in 2 Corinthians, Paul says, "working together with God." This can be misunderstood if an equal partnership with God is implied. We build the bridge from our side and God from his. When we meet in the middle, we congratulate each other for a job well done. Not so! The truth is far from an equal sharing of the responsibility for redemption.

An elephant and a flea once crossed a bridge which shook and swayed and all but broke under the tremendous weight. On the other side the flea said to the elephant, "We certainly shook that bridge." So the weight of our responsibility in the process of redemption is like the weight of a flea compared to that of an elephant.

Our role is to wait patiently while God builds the completed bridge to us. Then when he comes over to us, we surrender ourselves to him. We offer our lives as a living sacrifice. We open up our lives to him and he enters in and uses us to accomplish his redemptive work in our world. As Christ stepped into Peter's boat and took over, so Christ steps into our lives, and we open up, give up, and offer up our total selves to him.

Lost Grace

"That you receive not the grace of God in vain." This is the most difficult phrase in Paul's message, for it suggests the possibility that the grace of God, once received, proves ineffective and fruitless. However, a knowledge of Paul's theology would firmly assert that the grace of salvation, once given, can never be lost. Lost grace would be unthinkable to Paul. Since grace is the work of God in us, it cannot fail or come to nothing. In his letter to the Philippians Paul confidently assures them that the good work once begun in them would carry through to perfection until the day of Jesus Christ (Philippians 1:6).

Christ, himself, plainly affirms that his sheep, if given eternal life, shall never perish and no one shall snatch them out of his hand (John 10:28).

What then does Paul mean by "in vain"? Scholars offer many suggestions but one answer recommends itself, namely, to receive the grace of God in vain means that our *practice* does not measure up to our *profession*. When our lives deny what we say we believe, we have received grace in vain.

Christ died that we might no longer live for ourselves but to his glory. In Christ we are free from the Evil One, delivered from self-centeredness, restored to a right relationship with our God. When we live as if we are still Satan's slaves, thinking only of ourselves and ignoring our new relationship with God, then we are receiving grace in vain.

If a rich relative dies and leaves you an inheritance of a million dollars, and you still live like a pauper, then you are receiving this inheritance in vain. So with grace. It is God's loving legacy to us!

The Time Is Now

In Isaiah 61:2 the prophet speaks of "Jehovah's year of grace," and in 49:8 he speaks of a "season of acceptance." In the light of this prophecy Paul states that the gospel era is a season acceptable to God because it is the "day of salvation" appointed by God. Paul writes, "Now is the acceptable time." The acceptability of this time is dependent on God, not us. It is God who is giving us the opportunity of salvation by grace, now.

During World War I a U.S. officer sent an urgent wire: "Desperately need crossties. Move heaven and earth to get them to me by Saturday." General Charles G. Dawes, later Vice President of the United States, wired back: "Raised hell and got them today!"

Whenever Paul speaks of the day of redemption, there is this same note of urgency. His words are strong and cosmic. The *now* is a time of judgment. Heaven and earth are moved and hell is raised. All earthly existence is tense with expectancy and urgency. The heavens burst with hope. The burning possibility of hell is raised before us. The time is *now*! Now we are being saved. Now we are being ruined. Now the destiny of each of us is being decided according to the final and irrevocable standard of all judgment, Jesus Christ.

For Paul the coming day of judgment in the future, at the end of time, is not the beginning of judgment but the completion. Now this day of judgment begins in us. We stand between the cross-event and the End, between the inauguration of the Kingdom of God and its consummation when Christ comes in glory.

For those who are in Christ this is not bad news but good, because we who are in Christ have already been judged and are declared righteous before God.

Jesus Christ Superscar

If an epidemic of deadly disease broke out in your city and infected your family and you, and a doctor came to your house saying he had the antidote that would guarantee your and your family's cure, would you refuse? Would you turn your back on that doctor and say, "I want nothing to do with you. I will cure myself and my own family"? If so, you would be a fool.

Paul tells us that we are all victims of a deadly plague called Sin.

Then he adds, Jesus Christ comes to us from his cross on Calvary and shows us the scars in his hands and feet and side. He says to us, "From these scars flow forgiveness and life. Take them and you will be cured and live."

This is the good news! Christ provides the antidote, the cure for the deadly disease that infects us all and spells ruin and death for our lives. Why do we refuse?

Fulton J. Sheen said that young people today know Jesus Christ as Superstar. That is at least a beginning. But we need a more mature view of Christ. A superstar has a star on his dressing room door, but there is no star on our Lord's cross; there are only scars on his body. These scars proclaim the extent of God's love and the extent to which he is willing to go to forgive and love us. Fulton Sheen then adds that for us Jesus Christ is not superstar, but superscar!

This is the message of Paul. This is the gospel! Jesus Christ Superscar! And by his scars we are made clean, and whole, and new; we become the good friends of God.

A Sure Cure

First Sunday in Lent

Romans 5:12-19

This is a tough text. Many scholars identify this passage as one of the most difficult in all the New Testament. Therefore, it is important that at the beginning of our study we tie Paul down to his purpose at this point in his letter to the Romans. When we do, the whole passage lights up like a neon sign, declaring that Jesus Christ is the giver of God's free and unmerited gift of salvation to us all.

The method Paul uses in Romans 5:12-19 to accomplish this purpose is a series of contrasts between the work of Adam and the work of Christ, humanity under Sin compared with humanity under grace.

Although most scholars accept Paul's purpose and understand it, the thread of their thought becomes tangled when considering his method. The contrast Paul draws between Adam and Christ is so strange and unmanageable that many scholars dismiss it, or at least fence it in with parentheses. They agree with Luther that this passage is ''an entertaining outbreak and excursion'' and is not an important part of Paul's developed message to the Romans. It is Paul's acceptance of Adam as an historical figure that causes the problem. Scholars concur that here Paul is revealing that he is a man of his age, presenting the typical rabbinical view of Adam commonly held in his day. Paul did not have the advantage of modern research in science and anthropology which, according to modern scholarship, has proven there never was a first man, Adam. These scholars hold that the creation story of Genesis is not actual history but a cultic myth of the Hebrews.

Without taking sides on the validity of Paul's method, several things should be noted:

1. As a Jew, Paul would have accepted the story of Adam and Eve as a true record of creation. However, as a man of the first century, Paul would not have shared our interest in a scientific and critical view of history. Possessing an Eastern mind-set, he would

have been more interested in the *meaning of the story* than the factual details of this creation narrative.

2. Since Adam in the Hebrew language means "man" and represents the solidarity of the Jewish nation, there was a symbolic interest already built into the story. Therefore, Paul would have approached the story of creation as both a universal parable and a particular event of history. For Paul, Adam was both history and symbol.

Paul uses the Adam story to deal with the issue of how Sin entered our world, namely, by an act of disobedience. He is not concerned about proving the existence of Sin or the historicity of Adam. He is not saying that without Sin there would have been no Adam; nor is he saying without Adam there would have been no Sin. Paul does not question the existence of Sin in our world or of an Adam in history. These two figures are for Paul obvious realities. Paul does, however, desire to say something about the nature of Sin, namely, Sin is *universal*. Because Sin entered our world, all people are sinners.

Since in Paul's mind, Adam as the first man and the solidarity of humanity were accepted facts, his use of the Adam story was a most appropriate means of presenting the universality of Sin.

Justification

Paul has been dealing in his letter to the Romans with the issue of justification. As the word implies, it concerns justice. In the beginning chapters of Romans, Paul pictures God as bringing the gavel of divine justice down with a resounding blow, declaring all sinners are justified. To the legalists this is mind-blowing and Paul knew it. He knew that it was a shocking message to hear that a just and holy God would love and pardon sinful people and relate to them as his friends.

The response Paul gives to this reaction is "faith." "We have been justified through faith" (5:1). However, as Jeremias has pointed out, to understand this phrase in the Pauline sense, it should be stated "justified by Christ," or more precisely, "justified by the death and resurrection of Christ."

One for Many

The idea that one man could heroically die for others was not new or strange to Paul's readers. In the Maccabean wars in the early second century B.C., many innocent and pious Jews had been martyred for the safety of others.

Paul adds a new dimension to the idea of vicarious death. In the case of the heroic Maccabean martyrs, the beneficiaries of these sacrificial acts were always thought of as the good people of God. Pious people attempting to please God were thereby assisted in their efforts by the heroism of others. As Paul points out: "It may be that someone might die for a good person" (5:7b TEV). But Paul adds: "it was while we were still sinners that Christ died for us" (5:8b TEV). Then the additional clincher: "we rejoice in God through Jesus Christ, who has made us God's friends" (5:11b TEV).

This is radical! Sinners made friends with God while they still remain his enemies. How can this be? How can a *just* and *holy* God love and pardon sinful people and accept them as his friends? The passage which forms our lesson for the Second Sunday in Lent presents in a brief summary form Paul's complex answer to this question. This is why this passage, despite the fact that it is one of the most difficult in the New Testament, is at the same time one of the most important passages in Paul's writings.

An Outline of the Lesson

In Romans 5:12-19, Paul places the contrasts between Adam and Christ, sin and righteousness, death and life, against the background of three stages of religious history.

1. The age of Adam and the entrance of Sin and death into our world (5:12).

2. The age between Adam and Moses before there was the Law (5:13-14).

3. The age of Christ when the unrighteous are justified and made the friends of God (5:15, 17-19).

These three stages will form the outline of the discussion which follows. However, before proceeding with a detailed study of this outline, several basic presuppositions in Paul's theology should be considered.

The Difference Between an Individual and a Person

As noted above, the word Adam in the Hebrew language means "man" or "mankind." It was commonplace in Old Testament theology that the same word could represent an individual as well as a group — a society, a family, a race, a nation, a community. When Paul speaks of Adam, he does so in the light of this aspect of Jewish thought which could be summarized by the term, *solidarity*.

The Jew did not think of himself as an individual; he thought of himself as part of a group. Apart from that group he possessed no identity or real existence. It follows that a nation or race was not a collection of individuals but a single indivisible unit. What any individual did the nation did. Therefore, when one man, Adam, sinned, all society sinned.

Living as we do in a culture dominated by the idea of rugged individualism, it is difficult for us to understand the Jewish concept of social solidarity. Therefore, for this study it would be helpful to designate the two different views of human identity by using two different words. One view of identity will be designated by the word *individual* and the other by the word *person*.

1. **Individual.** To discover the identity of an individual it is necessary to separate and isolate the individual from the surrounding environment and from as many outside influences as possible. This is generally the way we Americans like to think about ourselves. We do not want our identity to be established by the race to which we belong; the creed we confess; or on what side of the tracks we were born; or how famous or infamous members of our family might have been or are. We want to be recognized as a unique "me." We say, "Take me as I am!"

This is also the approach of the scientists as they attempt to isolate and identify an element in chemistry or a virus in the bloodstream. Identity is discovered by separating and isolating the part from the whole.

2. **Person.** The identity of a person, on the other hand, is discovered not in a vacuum or in isolation but in *relationship*. How is the part related to the whole? This is the biblical view and the one held by the Jews. If you would know me as a *person*, you would have to know what kind of a son I am to my parents, what kind of a brother I am to my brothers and sisters, what kind of a husband I am to my wife, what kind of a father I am to my children, what kind of a friend I am to my friends. My true identity would be known in my total relationships to other people and to the things of this world.

This biblical view of personhood is not foreign to our experiences. Even though our culture claims allegiance and even obligation to the virtue of rugged individualism, "one lone man against the wilderness," practical experience suggests to us that the biblical view of *person* is often far more representative of how life is. In the words of the poet, "No man is an island." What one person does affects many.

For example: a man commits a crime, is caught and punished. Many suffer. He alone is guilty, but his family and friends, though completely innocent of the crime, also suffer.

Or a more common experience: Your neighbor neglects his lawn and the weeds flourish. No matter how hard you work to keep your front yard free of weeds, the winds blow the seeds of your neighbor's weeds onto your lawn and it is a losing battle.

Therefore, we need to keep in mind that as Paul writes his letters, he thinks in terms of the *person*, not an *individual*.

Sin and Sins

You may have noticed in our discussion so far that I have capitalized the word *Sin*. This is intentional and necessary because of the difference between Sin and sins in Paul's thought. Sin is a *state* or *condition* of our total self; sins are what we *do* because of the state or condition we are in.

Sin and sins. Sin is a *power* or force within our world greater than any single person or groups of persons. Sin is bigger than all society, and possesses a destructive potential mightier than the combined evil efforts of all humanity. As a power, Sin has the capacity to capture people and imprison them in its deadly grip. It might be compared to a disease or a virus which, like a plague, infects everything it touches. No person is immune to it.

This illness resulting from Sin separates us from God. It causes us to be self-centered rather than God-centered. It makes us proud, arrogant, independent, jealous, greedy, and exclusively self-serving and self-concerned. Even the good deeds we do are contaminated by Sin and only become means to our own betterment. All we do becomes sin. We are captured and are under the complete control of Sin. No part of us escapes. Sin holds our minds, our wills, our emotions, our actions in its vice-like grip.

In Romans 5:12-19 Paul is not so much concerned with sins and their forgiveness as much as he is with Sin as the demonic power which controls our lives. Our sins are only symptoms of our greater problem which is Sin. Sin is the culprit, the basic enemy of both God and us. What is needed, therefore, is not a change in what we do, but freedom from what *we are* because we are caught in the powerful grip of Sin. We do not need a moral reformation, but a total transformation, a complete change of the human condition, or as Jesus answered Nicodemus, we need "to be born again" and become a new person free from Sin.

The T.V. commercial shows a woman in distress about the condition of her husband's shirts. "That dirty ring around the collar. I try to wash it out, soak it out, scrub it out, but nothing seems to work." A little boy, seeing this commercial again and again, finally said to his mother, "Why doesn't that lady get her husband to wash his dirty neck?" A brilliant observation and solution, and from Paul's point of view very biblical. The ring around the collar is simply a symptom of a dirty neck. What needs washing is not the husband's shirt but his neck.

So with us. Sin soils us so that everything we do becomes dirty. Paul is not concerned with dirty laundry but with the fact that we are totally dirty. What we need is to be set free, to be resurrected out of our human condition and declared clean before God.

Death with a Capital D

For us death is an event at the end of life. The body dies and ceases to function physically; it returns to the earth and decays. Paul uses the word Death in a different sense. As Sin is a power, Death is a master. One of the greatest contrasts Paul speaks about in Romans is the contrast between Death, under whose power we stand by nature, and Life, which is given to us through faith in Christ.

According to Paul, Death came to hold sway over the world by means of Sin. Sin is the servant who goes ahead to prepare the way for Death. When, through Adam, Sin came into the world, the result was that Death came into control. Sin is the "sting of death" (1 Corinthians 15:56). Sin is the tool and weapon by which Death brought humanity under its power. Sin is the means by which Death got the human race in its grip, and now it is our real master. Death has ascended the throne of this world; and now with sovereign authority, it uses its power with terrifying effects. In the fifth chapter of Romans Paul repeats again and again, with increasing pointedness, that Death has attained to royal control in our world (5:14, 17, 21).

From the foregoing it follows that, for Paul, Death is not only an event which comes to us and puts an end to life; Death is a ruler controlling our total experience of living.

I. The Age of Adam and Entrance of Sin and Death

Came Into

Paul begins by acknowledging the fateful and fatal role played by our first father, Adam. It is a role of radical ruin for us all. Paul says: "Sin came into the world through one man" (5:12).

The important phrase here is "came into." The single point Paul is making is that Adam was the means by which Sin and Death entered into our world. There is no Original Guilt implied here. Paul does not say, as many of the doctors of the Church from Augustine on supposed him to say, "in whom all sinned" as though all of us sinned implicitly in Adam's sin and are therefore punished because of Adam's sin of disobedience. Paul does not say that we, as descendants of Adam, inherit a debt of sinfulness from Adam. Rather Paul states; "Sin came into the world through one man."

Following our analogy of Sin as a disease, Adam by his act of disobedience contacted and caught the deadly disease and contaminated the world with a black plague. Being human like Adam we are susceptible to the virus of Sin and Death and have no resistance. When we enter this world at birth, each of us is infected. The virus of Sin and Death spreads to every area of our being and because of this we commit sins. These wrong-doings are *our* sins, and therefore we are responsible for what we do even though we had nothing to do with the existence of the disease of Sin and Death's presence in our world. Adam is guilty for beginning the whole affair, but we are likewise guilty for carrying it on.

We are sinners both by *fact* and *act*. We are sinners because of the *fact* of Sin's presence in our world. We are sinners by *act* because, having been infected by Sin, we willfully commit immoral acts and live for ourselves alone, refusing to obey God's will for our lives.

The irony of our Sin-infected state is that we delude ourselves with the belief that we are in control; that we are free and can choose evil in one moment and good in another. The wrong-doings we commit are evidence that Sin is the power and Death is the master and we are but slaves. We try to save ourselves by looking out for "number one"; but all we do is useless; we still sin and die.

This may not seem fair to us. Paul would agree. The situation in which we find ourselves is not fair. That is precisely the point Paul is making. But it is not God's fault. Sin and Death are in power and they rule over us. We are in prison. Guilt or innocence is not the issue. The issue is our freedom. We need to get out of the situation in which we find ourselves. As things are, the cards are stacked against us and we cannot win. But, says Paul, I have good news for you. It is the good news of pardon, release, and freedom. God has not forsaken you. In Jesus Christ he comes with the power of grace which is greater than the combined powers of Sin and Death. On the cross God in Christ defeats Sin and Death, destroys their rule over us, and sets us free. God now takes over as ruler of our world, becomes our master, sets us free and gives us a new life in him.

The Ambition of Adam

There are several things that should be noted concerning the actions of Adam which created the situation in which we find ourselves.

1. Adam knew what he was doing. His was an act of disobedience not ignorance. He understood God had forbidden him to eat the fruit from the tree of good and evil. But he disobeyed. Adam was guilty because he "knew better."

2. Adam's action was not immoral, as we generally use and understand this term. He did not lie, cheat, or steal. He did not murder or commit adultery. What Adam did had nothing to do with "cigarets, wiskey and wild wild wimin." No! Adam sinned because he wanted to be as smart as God. Adam's act was not rebellion as much as it was ambition.

3. The phrase, "knowledge of good and evil," is frequently misunderstood. It is taken in the moral sense to know right from wrong. In the Old Testament the phrase "good and evil," taken together, is an idiomatic expression meaning "everything." Today we might say, "from A to Z." For example, in Genesis 31:24 to say "neither good nor evil" translates "to say nothing." In Zephaniah 1:12 "to do neither good nor evil" translates "to do nothing." To do good and evil means to "do everything." Other examples are Genesis 31:29 and 2 Samuel 13:22. Therefore, when the phrase "good and evil" is used in the creation story, it means "everything."

When we add to this the fact that "to know" in the Old Testament means "experience" (rather than intellectual perception), the complete phrase "knowledge of good and evil" translates "experience everything." When Adam was tempted to eat of the tree of the knowledge of good and evil, the Bible is saying that Adam was desiring to "experience everything." Adam literally wanted no limitations placed on his life. It was a desire to be God — his own God! It is not God's will that we should experience everything. Certain areas of life are God's province and certain experiences are God's prerogative and God's alone. Therefore, Adam's sin was not an immoral act but an act of ambition.

4. This is not a story about the origin of evil. Nor does it tell us where Sin came from. Before Eve came into the picture, evil and Sin were already present in the form of a serpent who possessed its own kind of cleverness. Where the sin-serpent with its evil ways came from, Genesis does not say, nor does Paul speculate. Paul is concerned with the real and actual presence of Sin and evil in our world, not their cosmic origin.

5. Having disobeyed God, Adam and Eve are on their own. They are driven from the garden. They have not trusted God so now they must trust their own cleverness to get along in a world separated from God. This is the beginning of society built on the foundation of ambition, which means independence, and disobedience, which spells exile from Eden.

On their own, what is the first thing that happens to Adam and Eve? They give birth to hatred and murder. Their son Cain kills his brother Abel in a fit of jealous rage and the crime of one person's inhumanity against another becomes the drama of life.

The conclusion drawn from this is that Adam and Eve, in their ambition and disobedience, became the parents of a family stained by hatred, greed, jealousy, and murder that made life on this earth one long, tragic-filled "soap-box opera." Into this family we are born, and we have about as much chance of pursuing happiness as a cellophane dog chasing an asbestos cat through hell.

A Sure and Certain Cure for Sin and Death

Paul uses Adam to witness how Sin and Death entered into our world and created the tragic situation in which we find ourselves. We are in big trouble. There is no doubt about that! We are slaves, prisoners, condemned to do evil and die. This only a blind and insensitive fool would deny.

Whether we accept the historicity of Adam or not, we cannot — we must not — discredit Paul's insights into the true nature of our human predicament just because he uses the example of Adam to witness the real presence of Sin and Death in our world. Paul's analysis and diagnosis of our tragic condition are brilliant no matter what method or images he uses to present them.

We are slaves to Sin and need a Savior. We are in prison and cannot free ourselves; we need a liberator. We are sentenced to die and need someone to pardon and free us. This is the bad news. We are helpless — totally helpless!

When we face and accept this we are prepared to hear the good news which is the primary purpose of Paul's message. The good news Paul brings is that our Savior, our liberator, our life-giver has come. God has sent his Son, Jesus Christ, to be our Savior and Lord. In him we have freedom, forgiveness, release, and redemption. In him we have a new and abundant life! Forever!

II. The Age Between Adam and Moses Before the Law Was Given

When we are in a hurry to cross town for an appointment, having to stop for a traffic light can be very irritating. But when we consider why the red light is placed there, we realize it is to enable us to arrive safely at our destination even though we may be late. Without these traffic regulations, every intersection would be a game of Russian roulette.

Paul speaks of a time when there was no law — the time between Adam and Moses. In this period people disobeyed God, but they didn't know it. Before the law, people were therefore not guilty, for guilt assumes the existence of a law and the willful disobeying of that law. As Paul says, "no account was kept of sins" (5:13 TEV). However, these people without a knowledge of sinning nevertheless died.

It is like the results of speeding on a slippery highway. Speed limits and traffic laws have nothing to do with the consequences of dangerous driving. If there are no traffic laws, you will not be arrested (your sins will not be counted against you); however, when you speed on the highway, hit a slick spot, lose control of your car, and crash head-on into a tree you will be just as dead whether there are traffic laws or not. Without traffic laws you will not be arrested, but you will not be safe from collisions that result in death.

This is what Paul is saying. Without the law you will not be charged and found guilty, but your wrong-doings will still result in a collision with death.

Innocent Children

The position of Paul concerning the absence of the law has something to say about how innocent children can be considered sinners. Children are in the same category as the people who lived between the time of Adam and Moses. Small children are too young to know the law, so for them it is as if the law did not exist. Therefore, they cannot be guilty of breaking the law. They can, however, act against God's will and thereby commit sins. They also share in God's judgment against a sinful society. Because of this they die.

Considering the analogy of Sin as a deadly virus which contaminates the world, the innocence of children would not protect them from catching the disease but might make them all the more susceptible.

The absence of the law, or the lack of knowledge of the law

according to Paul, means that we are not guilty, but this lack of guilt does not free us from the consequences of Sin in our world. Paul writes: "There was sin in the world before the Law was given; but since there was no law, no account was kept of sins. But from the time of Adam to the time of Moses death ruled over all men" (5:13-14a TEV).

III. The Age of Christ When the Unrighteous Are Justified and Made Friends of God

Finally, Paul makes a concluding contrast between Sin and grace, the old life in Adam and the new life in Christ.

The law was given, but it only served to increase trespassing. The law simply multiplied the possibilities of breaking God's commands by making us more aware. The situation is like that of the little boy who would never have been tempted by the freshly baked cookies if his mother had not told him to stay out of the cookie jar while she was gone.

With the law, sins increase, but, adds Paul, grace abounds even more. Sins are not insurmountable obstacles for God. They only challenge him to love us all the more. There is no darkness so dark that God cannot penetrate it with his light. There is no gulf so deep or wide that God cannot stretch forth his embracing arms and sweep us over to the safety of his side. For us this means that God's forgiveness is always greater than our capacity to sin. Despite the tragic conditions of our world, Paul is certain that God's grace will ultimately triumph.

We Are Better Off Than Adam

Paul says: "But how much greater is the result of what was done by the one man, Jesus Christ! All who receive God's abundant grace and the free gift of his righteousness will rule in life through Christ" (5:17 TEV). The "greater results" and "abundant grace" mean that Christ does not restore us to where we were before the Fall. He has done so much more for us. He takes us to a state far beyond the innocence of Adam. We are given a new and abundant life. This new life, Paul says, "abounds."

This means we are not simply *forgiven*, but given a great gift. We are given a state of existence which is superior to that of Adam. Adam was innocent. Innocence suggests the lack of something. Adam was made by God from the dust of the earth. He was made in God's image, but Adam was, as it were, *outside* the life of God. He was a creature above all other creation, but he was still not a child of God. However, "in Christ," we become more than creatures possessing the image of God; we become children of God. We are no longer outside but *inside* the household of God.

Not on Probation

What does this mean for us? Adam was made in the image of God, innocent; nevertheless Adam was on probation. He possessed the capacity and possibility of falling from grace and of being separated from God. Adam fell and was driven from the garden and thereby separated from his creator.

"In Christ" we are not in a state of probation. There is no possibility of our falling from grace. We are baptized by the blood of the cross and the power of the Holy Spirit. This act declares us to be adopted sons and daughters of the living God. No matter what we do, this relationship cannot be lost, for it is not a relationship which we create but which Christ creates. Our baptism and adoption are a once and for all event. Christ's death for us was final and unrepeatable. Of this Paul is absolutely certain, and Christ himself has said: "No man shall be able to pluck them out of my Father's hand" (John 10:29 KJV). The certainty of this new life in Christ is the "much more" of which Paul speaks. Adam was on probation. Adam's destiny had a big question mark behind it. Our life in Christ is an absolute certainty with an exclamation point before and after it.

What If We Sin Tomorrow?

This free and unmerited gift of grace and life seem too good to be true, so we inevitably ask, "But what if we sin tomorrow?" Will tomorrow's sins change or alter our standing before God? Will we lose this new life? Will we go back to "being in Adam," the old life? Paul's answer is, "No!" Salvation is not a revolving door — being "in Christ" today and "in Adam" tomorrow. In Christ there is no going back.

We can never again be imprisoned by Sin and Death. We will die as all creatures die, but we will survive the experience of death and will never be separated from God. Through the worst of times, we shall remain the children of God, for what Christ gives us cannot be taken from us. What Christ gives is not a sinless life but a victorious life.

Nor do we go back to being under the law. In Christ we are free from the law forever, "old things have passed away; behold, all things are become new" (2 Corinthians 5:17 KJV).

This does not mean that we are to find comfort in a life lived contrary to God's will. Rather we are to strive in every way to please God and do his will. But when we *fail*, we do not *fall*. For we do not sin against the law; we sin against *love*. We sin not as hard criminals but as loved children, and that is the decisive difference.

When we sin we do not break a law; we break our Father's heart. God grieves when we sin against him, but he does not disown us. The certainty of our status in the family of a loving Father is Paul's central message. He repeats it again and again. In chapter eight of his letter to the Romans, he rises to poetic expression of this certainty.

> *If God is for us, who can be against us? Certainly not God, who did not even keep back his own son, but offered him for us all . . . Who, then can separate us from the love of Christ? Can trouble do it, or hardship or persecution or hunger or poverty or danger or death? . . . No, in all these things we have complete victory through him who loved us! For I am certain that nothing can separate us from his love: neither death nor life; neither angels or other heavenly rulers, or powers; neither the present or the future; neither the world above nor the world below — there is nothing in all creation that will ever be able to separate us from the love of God which is ours through Christ Jesus our Lord (8:31b-32a, 35, 37-39 TEV).*

How much more strongly could Paul declare the certainty of our state of salvation in Christ than this? Who could in the light of these words ask, ''Can we fall from grace?''

But you say, ''Is this not dangerous? Is this not an open invitation for us to go out and live it up — committing every kind of wrong-doing with gusto and delight?'' No! For when we are truly in Christ, we are in love, and those who are in love do not think that they are now free to do anything *they* please but strive above all else to please their lover.

So we who are truly in Christ are so enthralled and thrilled with our new relationship that we are filled with sheer joy and will spare no effort to please and be worthy of so great a gift.

Christ gives us the gift of falling in love with God — or better said — rising to a new life in God's love. We literally rise to new heights of endeavor to please our loving father, not because we must but because we want to. And in Christ we can!

As Christians our first responsibility is to rejoice. But this is the point where we so often fail. We fail to be the joy-filled friends of

God. Today the greatest evangelistic message we can proclaim is not John the Baptist's message, "repent and return," but Paul's message, "realize and rejoice." Realize what Christ has done for us and rejoice in it!

For too long a time the Church has represented itself to the world as a grim-faced moralist, sternly warning the world to repent from its sins and turn back to God. This is a legitimate message when people are rejoicing and celebrating the accomplishments and achievements of their self-made world. But this is not the mood of our times. All about us is despair! Nations stockpile weapons of nuclear destruction and live in constant fear that some foolhardy leader will push the button and it will all be over. We have lost our pride and faith in technology and science. The utopia they promised only buries us deeper in pollution and drives us onto wastelands raped of all natural resources. We are disillusioned because we are convinced there can be no abiding relationships of love. Stress, depression, suicide, divorce, poverty, starvation, and corruption dominate our language and hypnotize our thoughts.

Therefore, the time has come for us who are in Christ to present a new face to the world — the joy-filled face of loved children, the joy-filled face of those who live in the absolute certainty of Christ's love and redemption. Even though the world has turned its face away from God, he has not turned his face away from us! God has not forsaken his world! He has given his Son as a ransom for it! In the death and Resurrection of Jesus Christ, our Lord, God has freed this world from the power of Sin and Death and has given to all people the opportunity of a new and abundant life! Paul shouts forth to a world sick unto death: "We rejoice in God through our Lord Jesus Christ, who made us God's friends!"

Righteousness Is Not for Sale

Second Sunday in Lent

Romans 4:1-5, 13-17

Today most of us are by necessity cost conscious. And we have a right to be with inflation, the devalued dollar, and ever-increasing taxation. Our income fails to measure up to our out-go. Therefore, we want to know the cost of everything before we buy it and the demands of a deal before we buy into it.

We all talk about the high cost of everything; but the interesting thing is that when the price is too low we become suspicious. Low cost seems to imply that a thing is poorly made or constructed of inferior materials. We wonder if there are not hidden costs or small print ignored on the bottom line of the contract. Ever since the Trojan Horse we have heard it said, "Beware of Greeks bearing gifts."

The same reactions occur when we start talking about the requirements of redemption. If the cost of heaven and the demands of salvation are too cheap and easy, we become suspicious. The teaching that salvation is a free and unmerited gift is met with stiff opposition and objections, especially from the legalists and the moralists. For them the punishment of hell and the rewards of heaven are absolutely necessary if any system of religion is going to work. Righteousness must have its price!

Paul confronted this reaction from the Jews of his day. Their religion was built on the strict agreement between God and his people. God is holy and just. He punishes the wicked and rewards the righteous. The cost of righteousness is obedience. The rewards of righteousness come only to those who pay the price by obeying the law and doing God's whole will. Paul's witness stood in direct contrast to this salvation by good works and obedience to the law. For Paul righteousness is not for sale! It is a gift!

Good Works and Faith

In Romans 4:1 Paul points to Father Abraham. This was a wise approach. As George Washington was the father of our country, so for the Jews, Abraham was the father of their nation. He personified for them the three basic pillars of their religious conviction, Law, Works and Merit.

Like a New Testament Samson, Paul pulls down the pillars of the temple of Jewish thought and replaces them with his own big three, Promise, Faith and Grace. The basis for this attack against the Jewish beliefs is, surprisingly, Abraham. For Paul, Abraham personifies not Law but Promise, not Works but Faith, not Merit but Grace.

Paul begins his offensive by agreeing with the Jews that Abraham was *the* righteous man, the prototype of all the faithful, the superstar of righteousness. Then Paul poses the crucial question as to what made Abraham *the* righteous man of history.

Was it obedience? Everybody knows that Abraham was an obedient man. When God told him to pack up his family and go to a new and strange land, Abraham went! When God demanded the sacrifice of his son, Abraham did not withhold the knife but raised it in absolute obedience.

Yes, Abraham was an exceptional man. He certainly had much to boast about before men; but how about before God? That is something else. Before God, Abraham was as ungodly as any other man. For Paul the record is clear. Abraham was righteous because of his faith, not because of his good works of obedience. Paul quotes Genesis 15:6, "Abraham believed God, and because of his faith God accepted (reckoned) him as righteous" (4:3 TEV).

Had Abraham been justified by his works, the Scriptures would have given an entirely different account. They would have said that the good done by Abraham was the means by which he achieved righteousness. However, the Scripture ignores everything Abraham had done and mentions only his faith. Paul's conclusion is that only the believer is righteous before God, as it is written concerning Abraham.

Reckoned

The key word in Genesis 15:6 is *logidzomai* which is translated in most cases as "reckoned." God reckoned him as "righteous." The Good News translation uses the word "accepted." "God accepted Abraham as righteous." The Greek word *logidzomai* comes from the accountant's vocabulary in the world of business. It means to "calculate, compute, credit, to enter on record, to put to one's account." Literally what is being said here is that God opened the Record Book of Life and wrote down after Abraham's name "a righteous man." God made the notation "righteous," not because of Abraham's good works of obedience, but because of his faith. Faith was the decisive issue on Abraham's record.

Paul attacks good works on several grounds: (1) Boasting, (2) Wages Earned, (3) God's Freedom.

1. Boasting (Romans 4:2)

The accomplishment of good works brings self-satisfaction and leads to pride and boasting. A proud and boastful person has no need of a savior. Good works, therefore, result in satisfaction but not salvation.

Helen Hayes, the great actress, said her mother drew the distinction between achievement and success. Her mother advised her that "achievement is the knowledge that you have studied and worked hard and done the best that is in you. Success is being praised by others, and that's nice, too, but not so satisfying."

There is no place in the process of salvation for a sense of self-achievement or public success. In Paul's mind both are deadly dangerous. God cannot give a gift to an achiever, or a person made proud by success; God can give gifts only to the humble and lowly who in their helplessness cry out to him for mercy.

The National Weather Service advises that if you are caught out in the open during a severe lightning storm you should kneel down, bend forward, and put your hands on your knees. What you are doing is maintaining a low profile. This is what Paul is saying regarding our stance before God; we should at all times in our relationship with God maintain a low profile.

2. Wages Earned (Romans 4:4)

Paul argues that when a person works for something the reward received is a wage; but if something is received without working for it, then it is a gift. It follows that good works result in a wage; belief receives righteousness as a gift.

For Paul, good works by their very nature exclude both faith and grace. Faith cannot exist where there is a feeling of merit, "I deserve this." The people who believe good works *save* trust only in their own works and in themselves, not in God. Faith, on the other hand, distrusts everything and clings only to God.

On Christmas morning Johnny received the bicycle he had desperately wanted. He knew that he had not been good and, therefore, didn't deserve it. When he mentioned this to his parents, his father answered, "Son, we didn't give you this bicycle because you have been good, but because we love you." This is the true spirit of giving, and for Paul, this is the basis of God's giving. He gives not because we are good, but because he is good and loving.

3. God's Freedom (Romans 4:14)

Good works are also ruled out because they tend to place God in our debt. God becomes obligated to us. When we attempt to pile up credits of good works and then present these good works to God, saying, "Look at all the good things I have done," we are more interested in ourselves than we are in God. We inevitably use God to serve our own ends. God becomes little more than a master of ceremonies who on the final days awards trophies to winners.

God is God. If he is to be God, then he must be free to act as he wills. God can never be obligated or bound to do anything for us except what he chooses to do. If God shows us any favor, it is because he desires to do it, not because he is legally or morally bound to do it. Good works put both God and us under the law. The law dictates to God what is just and good, and God is no longer the free judge of all creation; he is only a policeman enforcing laws, issuing moral traffic tickets, and punishing violators.

Is Faith a Good Work?

What then of faith? If faith is an act of belief, does it not become another kind of good work which must be done in order to merit righteousness? Paul would answer "definitely not" for several reasons:

1. Faith is a work of God, not of our doing. Faith is a gift. Faith is what happens when God is at work in us. When electricity passes through a fluorescent tube, a glow is given off. So when God works in us and through us, a glow is given off. This glow, this light, we call faith. The tube can give off no glow and produce no light without electricity passing through it. So with faith, it is the product not of our doing but is a work of God in us.

2. Faith did not make Abraham a good man. God only declared him to be good and righteous. Paul makes this clear in 4:6 (not included in our lesson) where the author of Psalms is quoted concerning the happiness of the man whom God accepts as righeous, apart from *any* work:

How happy are those whose wrongs
God has forgiven,

Whose sins he has covered over!
How happy is the man whose sins
the Lord will not keep account of! (Psalm 32:1-2)

God does not erase our sins but covers them up (literally hides them) when he declares us to be righteous. We are not *made* righteous, only declared so. There is no evidence that we are righteous. We have only God's word that it is so. Therefore, we can only trust God's good word.

3. Faith, if it is true faith, always points to another. It never calls attention to itself, as good works do. The characteristic that makes faith *faith* is that it does not consider its actions to be good works. It claims nothing for itself. Faith acknowledges total helplessness. Faith places all its weight upon another.

A young African, when climbing a palm tree to get coconuts, will place a knife in his teeth and a woven strand of vine-rope around his waist. This rope is much like the safety belts of telephone linemen. The climber leans back on the rope and carefully climbs the high tree, cuts the fruit and descends using the same rope around his waist. A tourist asked one of these young men if the method he used was really safe. "It is," answered the young man, "if you trust the rope enough to put all your weight on it."

So with faith. The weight of all merit and accomplishment needs to be placed squarely, completely and totally on God.

The Promise and Faith

We learned in the previous lesson that because of Adam's disobedience, Sin and Death came into the world and established rule over it. Now God gives to Abraham a promise, addressed not just to Abraham, but to all people. The promise is that God will restore his kingdom. God will drive Sin and Death from their positions of power and will establish himself as ruler and Lord of this world. Those who are made righteous by faith will share in this new kingdom. God will be their God and all people will be his people.

God gave the Law to the Jewish people; but it is not the gift of the Law that makes persons the chosen people. Rather is it the *promise* given by grace and received by faith that makes a person *chosen*. The Law never gives a promise. The Law never gives anything. It can only mete out justice. The Law does not deal in trust but in violations. It does not offer an inheritance but a penalty. The Law cannot give hope, only terror; not a promise, but death.

The Law is conditional. It can only say, "If you do this, then you will receive salvation." But the tragic truth is that we soon discover that we cannot fulfill the Law. Try as we may, we fall far short of the Law's demands.

At our best we are like the little boy who came home with his grades. He proudly presented them to his father. "You look as if you passed arithmetic," the father remarked. "No," answered the son, "but I did make the highest grade of those who failed!" So with us. In the test of the Law, the best we can do is make the highest grade of those who fail. If our future depends on our fulfilling the Law, then we are a people without hope.

On the other hand, the promise of God is a certainty, for it is an action of God, not our action. As the Scriptures states, "I have made you father of many nations." God does not say to Abraham, "I will make you father of many nations, if you believe, or if you do good works." God says, "I have made you . . ."

The sequence of this action is essential:

1. God gives the promise.
2. The promise enables Abraham to believe and have faith.
3. Because of the faith born of promise within Abraham, he is declared righteous.

God is the mover. The whole process of redemption is God's action. Abraham is the receiver of the promise, the faith and the righteousness. Abraham has no reason to boast; only in gratitude and thanksgiving can he build an altar to the Lord and cry out, "Thanks be to God who does *all* things well!"

Faith Is Not Blind

One of the reasons why faith so often becomes a virtue in our minds, and thereby a good work rather than a gift, is the common fault of thinking faith is blind. We view faith as determination to close our eyes to the impossible, the improbable, even the absurd. Faith is believing despite all the negative evidence.

Paul, however, does not stress faith as blind, human determination to believe despite all odds. Paul does not say that Abraham believed the impossible, the improbable, the absurd. Rather, Paul says that Abraham believed because of God's *promise*.

Since Abraham had God's promise, he could not be made to doubt God even though he saw clearly that his human resources were not equal to its fulfillment. This is the faith for Paul — to hold to God's promise and not close one's eyes to reality, to see clearly that the promise of God is the only sure foundation on which to build one's life, even if all human calculations contradict.

When God told Abraham that he was to be the father of many nations, Abraham's first reaction was to take this promise in the physical sense of being the father of many children. Abraham knew he had no children and was too old to hope for any. His wife Sarah was ninety years old and could no longer conceive one child, let alone many. What God was promising was, therefore, humanly impossible. God, however, had a far greater meaning in mind. Abraham was to be the father of all who believe and are thereby made righteous.

Later, God does promise Abraham that physically he will have a son by his wife Sarah. When Abraham heard this he "fell upon his face and laughed" (Genesis 17:17). After all, he was one hundred years. And when Sarah, who was ninety, heard it, she too laughed (Genesis 18:12). Then follows a delightful little drama. God said to Abraham, "Why did Sarah laugh?" Sarah, hearing this, denied it saying, "I didn't laugh!" God then turns to Abraham and repeats his promise: "Is anything too hard for the Lord? At the time appointed I will return to you, in the spring, and Sarah shall have a son."

The point here is clear. You don't doubt God's word of promise; nor do you laugh at it. God is serious! What God says will happen — does happen! It is, therefore, God's word and not our faith that is fundamental. The promise given in God's word possesses the power to accomplish the deed. Therefore, when we hear the story of Abraham's faith, our reaction should not be, "What a man of faith!" but "What a God!" This is the point Paul is making when he refers to Abraham's faith, namely, the word God speaks in his promise is so powerful that when God speaks, Abraham believes.

According to Paul this is why Abraham was declared to be a righteous man — because God gave him a promise. So with us; it is not by *our* faith that we are declared righteous, but by God's word and God's promise which create faith within us. Thus God is glorified, not us! Faith is not blind, but sees the power of God's word at work in all of life, and sees God's promise fulfilled in Jesus Christ, our Lord.

All across our country there are giant pylons that carry electricity from power plants into distant cities. The high tension wires carry a voltage far too great to be harnessed and used for our human necessities. Before it can be used to light our homes, clean our carpets, wash our clothes, toast our bread, it must be transformed into a lower voltage suitable for normal uses of human life. So the original promise of God to his people is a great distance of thousands of years from us. It was uttered in a strange land to people far removed from us; but in Jesus Christ this promise of God became incarnate in the flesh of our daily lives. Jesus Christ, the living Lord, is God's mighty transformer. He brings the power of God's promise down into the terms of our needs and makes this inheritance accessible to our faith. Therefore, like Abraham, our faith is founded not in ourselves but in our God!

Let Your Light Shine

The Third Sunday in Lent

Ephesians 5:8-14

If you were to stand in space, the distance of the sun to the earth and do two things — say a word and light a candle, theoretically in eight minutes the people on earth would see the light of the candle, but they would not hear the word for more than a day, over thirty-two hours. This is because sound is so much slower than light, which suggests that the weakness of much Christian witness is that we would rather talk than shine.

We start out in Sunday school singing, "This little gospel light of mine, I'm gonna let it shine." But so soon our faith loses its luster. It becomes tarnished by indifference and neglect. And when faith loses its sparkle, it is no longer attractive to us or to others. It is a dull, dismal, and dreary thing of the intellect only. Faith becomes creeds and confessions, dogmas and doctrines. Our churches become lecture halls and our worship becomes talkathons that test our endurance to listen. For many, the sermon is the Protestant form of penance, something suffered through once a week to satisfy the requirements of being a member of the church. Faith and religion are a burden we bear to assure our eternal salvation.

How different is the view of Paul as he writes in Ephesians 5:8-14, "you are light in the Lord." He talks about faith as an exhilarating experience of coming out of a cave of darkness into the bright warming light of the sun. Our new life in Christ, far from being a dull and dreary one, is exciting and joyfilled; rather than a burden, it is a blessing.

Paul says something more to us. He does not say that we are children of light, or that we are to walk in the light, he says we *are* light. It is one thing to say that we merely walk in light; it is quite another to say we are light. To *be* light means that everywhere we are there is light. For light is not something outside ourselves that we need to search for, or struggle to remain in; rather light is within us. When we enter into lives that are filled with the darkness of sorrow or suffering, distress or disappointment, emptiness or meaninglessness, we come bringing light. We literally light up their lives.

Works — Fruit

According to Paul, as light, we are productive and produce the good fruit of goodness, righteousness, and truth. The use of the word "fruit" rather than "works" is helpful here, for in our everyday use of words there is a difference between "work" and "fruit." Work refers to a process that produces something. Fruit is the product that is produced.

Work carries with it the idea of exerted effort, heavy labor, something we must do in order to get what we want. The alarm clock rings us awake. It's another day — another work day. We would rather remain in the warmth and comfort of our bed. But no! We must get up and go to work. After all, we have to eat, feed and clothe our family, pay bills and taxes, and all this demands work.

When we hear the word "work," we think of tools and toil; we smell sweat and factory fumes; we hear time clocks and quitting whistles. We think of piece-work on assembly lines, secretaries at typewriters, men in grey flannel suits with briefcases rushing to catch the morning commuter, beds to be made, dishes to be washed, and kids to be taxied all over town. The atmosphere that surrounds the word "work" is negative, obligatory, a burden to be born.

However, the atmosphere that surrounds the word "fruit" is positive, free and joyous. There is about it the glimmer of golden orange groves in the warm Florida sunshine, red apples ripening in the fresh fall winds of a Virginia valley, rich grapes bending the vines in southern California, bountiful harvests of grain carpeting the fields in the midwest. It is something to celebrate and sing about. It is time to gather the fruits of our labor and thank God for his beautiful, life-giving blessings.

For Paul no good works on our part are required for salvation. God is the worker of the one good work necessary for our salvation; this he accomplishes in the life and death of his son, Jesus Christ. The sweat of salvation's work drops from the brow of our savior as blood. The tired and aching muscles of redemption's toil hang from a cross nailed there by our sins. This is God in Jesus Christ doing the work of our salvation for us. This is the good work that makes all our good works ineffective and unnecessary.

For us remains the fruit. Our lives are to be active; we are to produce not works but fruit. What we do does not produce salvation but is the product of our salvation. God has done the good work necessary for our salvation. He has accomplished our salvation in Christ. Now it is for us to reap the harvest in lives lived as light in the world.

Paul as Pastor

Many scholars are concerned that Paul in this section of Ephesians becomes moralistic. In chapters 1-3 of Ephesians, Paul comes across as the great theologian propounding his doctrine of the cosmic Christ who will heal every division in God's universe and unite the whole creation in himself. Then in the first part of Chapter 4, Paul assumes the role of church statesman, telling us of our essential unity in Christ, our functional diversity in the church, and the goals of our Christian obedience. Then from the heights of theology and ecclesiology Paul seems to bring us down with a bump to the level of authoritarian, puritanical, old-fashioned, narrow-minded, negative morality.

Granted, this is not like Paul at all. In fact, that is not what he is doing. He is not here assuming the role of an authoritative disciplinarian; rather he is revealing his essential nature as a pastor. Paul does not deal in this fifth chapter of Ephesians with cold legalistic rules that must be obeyed under the threat of punishment. Rather, he is counseling and comforting his people. He is not telling them what they *must* do, but what they *can* do and *will* do because they are new people in Christ.

Once we were darkness. Now we are light. Paul is describing what it means to be light. He presents the fruits of light as goodness, righteousness and truth. "For the fruit of light is found in all that is good and right and true" (5:9).

Goodness — Kindness

The first fruit of light is goodness. The Greek word here is *agathosune*, which is more helpfully translated "kindness," for it means to be compassionate, congenial, well-disposed toward others.

Our English word "kindness" comes from the stem *kin* from which we get our word "kindred" or family. Literally, what Paul is saying is that we are to treat all people as if they were our own "kin-folks" — our own family.

Right — Rights of Others

The second fruit of light is "right" or "righteousness." The Greek word is *dikaiosune*, which literally means "giving to men and God that which is their due." The implication of the word means more than giving what is due; it means expressing an attitude that you are "happy to do far more than is required by mere justice." It suggests the teaching of Jesus, "If a man desires you to go a mile with him, go with him two." *Dikaiosune* is service as God serves, giving more than is asked or expected.

True — Sincere

The third fruit of light is "true" or "truth." The Greek word here is *aletheia*, which is not simply an intellectual thing to be grasped with the mind, but implies sincerity, genuineness, the absence of sham or pretense.

Style of Life

It is obvious that the fruits of light — kindness, consideration of others, and sincerity — are not rules and regulations that present precise directives for every situation that may arise in life; rather they are guidelines of conduct that lead to a distinctive style of life. For Paul the essence of Christian obedience is not keeping certain rules, but a style of life that reflects obedience to the living presence of Christ and the development of an intuitive sense in each unique situation of what action-response would gain Christ's approval.

This does not mean that we strive to imitate Christ. There are many situations in which we find ourselves today that are so different from the issues Christ faced that we have no example or even a basis for comparison. For example, the social issues of abortion, life-sustaining machines, cloning, etc., are never mentioned in the Scriptures. However, it does not follow that when faced with such issues, we are on our own. Christ is with us at all times. He is ready to direct our decisions and actions. We turn to him and struggle, even agonize with his instructive guiding presence in our lives, praying that he would reveal what would be pleasing to him.

When life's directives depend on an interpretation and application of general rules and regulations, we do not need a living God. He could die and we could get along just fine, as long as he left behind for our instruction a last will and testament of his will that could be followed to the letter. On the other hand, if there are no legal directives, no complete commandments for every situation, then we need a living Lord to walk with us every step of the way into every given situation. Without this living presence and guidance of our Lord, we would be utterly lost.

Once there was a man who dreamed he was walking on the beach with the Lord. As the two of them walked along, scenes from the man's life began to appear before him. In these scenes there were two sets of footprints; one belonging to the Lord, the other belonging to the man. But as more scenes appeared, the man noticed that in some of them there was only one set of footprints. He began to realize these scenes were always the most painful and struggle-filled times in his life. So he decided to ask the Lord about them. "Lord," he said, "when I gave you charge of my life, you promised to be always with me, to guide and strengthen me all along the way. Why, then in these times when I needed you most, were you not there?" The Lord smiled and said, "My friend, you know that I love you so much that I would never leave you to face life alone. Those scenes where you saw only one set of footprints, those were the times I was carrying you!"

This is Paul's approach to the Christian style of life. We are light because we are in the light which is Christ. He is with us and we are with him. In the toughest of times he will carry us, direct, instruct, and grant us the power of insight into what is God's will in any moment of decision. At the same time he will give us the strength to accomplish it. This is the style of life Paul prays will be ours.

Learn by Doing

"And try to learn what is pleasing to God." (5:10) The Greek text here makes it clear that Paul is stressing that intellectual knowledge of God's will is not enough. Rather we are to throw ourselves — our whole selves — into the process of knowing God's will.

The Bible has no word for our English term "experience." If it did, Paul might have written, "Find out by experience what is pleasing to the Lord." There are many things best learned by experience. This is particularly true of skills; driving a car, dancing, public speaking are all best learned by doing. All sports demand involvement of the total person — body, mind and will — if they are to be learned and mastered. For Paul, living is an art, a skill, a sport, carrying with it the excitement of expressing yourself and the joy of doing something well. The good life for Paul is not something we do grudgingly, pressured by someone else to do something we don't want to do. Who could imagine pressuring a teenager to learn to drive a car? Teenagers cannot wait until they reach the age when their life can gain its wheels. In our contemporary, secular culture the driving of a car solo is the maturity-rite, the confirmation-sacrament of adulthood. It is the moment every young person dreams of and anxiously awaits. So for Paul the moral life is not forced obligation but that for which we anxiously wait. It is the moment when we can leave the awkward adolescent way of living and become an adult living a mature life style. The fruit of light is the natural result of our spontaneous desire to be the mature person we were intended to be. Live by the light and you will discover the fun and thrill of doing good before God.

Pleasing to God

The most meaning-filled word in this statement is the word "pleasing." Here is the key to understanding Paul's view of moral maturity — that which is "pleasing to God."

Mother tries to get Johnny to take a bath, comb his hair, and brush his teeth. She lays down the law and literally wears herself out trying to enforce it. Then one day she discovers Johnny bathed and dressed in his best disco-shirt, standing in front of the mirror combing and re-combing his hair. What has happened? What caused this moral transformation? Johnny is in love. His whole purpose in life has become one dedicated campaign to please the blue-eyed blond in his history class.

What mother had tried so hard to accomplish with the law, Johnny is doing on his own. But not really on his own, for someone has come into his life. He has become the captive of love. His one desire is to please the love that has taken hold of him.

This is Paul's view of the redeemed life. When God's love for us comes to realization in our life, we fall in love with God. Or as previously stated, "rise in love," for being in love with God lifts us up to ever higher levels of living. The motivating power of the good life, the life that is "light," therefore, becomes the desire above all else to please God. Any other reason for the good and moral life is artificial and ultimately self-defeating.

The Death of Dracula

Paul then points out that we are to "take no part in the unfruitful works of darkness, but instead expose them." (5:11) This passage has been interpreted in several ways. It all depends on how one understands the word "expose." The Greek word used here can be translated "rebuke" or "convict" which would suggest a verbal denunciation of evil. This brings to mind a picture of little old ladies in tennis shoes peeking out of their windows at the antics of their neighbors, gossiping on the telephone, and running around all over town on a moral crusade, condemning all evil with bitter tongues.

However, more is meant here than verbal protest. Evil is to be more than exposed; it is to be actively opposed. Something needs to be done about it. The picture suggested is more like that of the horror classic *Dracula*. Protesting the evil of Dracula, the prince of darkness is not enough; you need to find his hiding place — the coffin filled with his native soil — and then open the lid to his coffin and let the light of day fall upon and expose his figure. This act of exposure to the light ends the curse of Dracula and he decomposes into dust and is no more.

So we are to expose the unfruitful works of darkness by opposing them with light. It is not enough to talk about evil, we need to actively expose it to the light and thereby oppose and destroy it.

Darkness Becomes Light

In Paul's mind the destruction of evil is not like the *Dracula* classic at all points. When Dracula is destroyed he decomposes and is no more. That is the end of the story. When light exposes evil and destroys it, this is not the end. In verse 13 Paul writes, "When anything is exposed by the light it becomes visible, for anything that becomes visible is light." Evil is destroyed by becoming light. Lincoln once said that the only way to destroy enemies is to make friends of them. This is Paul's answer to the destruction of evil. It is transformed into light. When you walk into a room filled with darkness and light a lamp, the darkness becomes light.

In verse 8 Paul says of us, "Once you were darkness, but now you are light." Now in verse 13 he is talking about those who came in contact with us. As light we expose the darkness of evil and destroy it. We literally light up the lives of those who dwell in the darkness of evil. As once we were turned from darkness into light, so all who come in contact with us are turned from darkness into light.

Baptismal Hymn

Verse 14 is introduced as a quotation. "Awake, O sleeper, and arise from the dead, and Christ shall give you light." Most scholars suggest this is a quotation from an early baptismal hymn, perhaps sung at the moment the convert came out of the water. It is more than likely based on Isaiah 60:1, "Arise, shine; for your light has come, and the glory of the Lord has risen upon you."

Whatever its origin, Paul is here giving us an example of the way reproof is to be administered to those who are in darkness. Our reproof of wrong-doers is to take the form of an urgent call to let the light of Christ shine on them. Its aim is not to rebuke, condemn or judge; rather we are to seek the conversion and transformation of sinners. It is also Paul reminding us that the change of darkness into light is not our doing but a work of Christ in and through us.

We could as light become noisy busybodies, taking pleasure in discovering and revealing evil, thereby enhancing our own superior achievements in right living. There is always the demonic temptation of making ourselves look good by exposing the worst in the life of others. Paul, however, makes it quite clear that this is not our role as light in a dark world. Rather we are to permit Christ to use our light to bring others to the joy of being light instead of darkness. Our light is a witness that, like the rising sun, should awaken people to the fact that Jesus Christ is the true light. In him a new day has dawned. As we are in him and he is in us, we are light. By this light we are possessed. As the wick of a candle we burn ourselves up, witnessing to the light which has set our lives on fire.

One evening a young man, frantically searching for a thrill, decided to race a train to the crossing. It was an exact tie and the young man lost. His family decided to sue the railroad because no warning was given at the crossing. An officer of the railroad went to the watchman involved and asked if he was on duty at the time of the accident. Did he take his lantern and wave it as a warning to motorists of the approaching train? The watchman stressed he was not derelict. He was on duty. He waved his lantern in warning, but the young man ignored it and raced to the crossing.

At the trial the lawyers placed the watchman on the witness stand and examined him, "Were you there?" The watchman shouted "Yep!" Then the lawyer shook his finger in the watchman's face. "Did you wave your lantern as a warning?" "Yep!" came the reply. Again and again the lawyers examined and cross-examined him but the old watchman stuck to his story.

The case against the railroad was dismissed. Afterwards the railroad officials called the watchman into the main office. "We were afraid," they said, "that you might back down and admit you weren't there." The watchman answered, "No. I was there, but I got a little nervous during the trial because I was afraid one of them smart city lawyers was going to ask me if my lantern was lit!''

It makes all the difference whether or not the lantern was lit. So in the area of Christian service and living. Much that is accepted as Christian living and witness is the waving of unlit lanterns. It is only following rules and regulations in a habitual sort of way, a style of living that is routine and regular but which lacks light — the enthusiastic joy of those who are on fire for Christ.

Paul says, "once you were darkness, now you are light." If that gift of light Christ gives us does not shine in and through us, then our lives mean little more than waving unlit lanterns in unending darkness.

Safe! The Game Is Won!

Fourth Sunday in Lent

Romans 8:1-10

The score is tied. It is the last of the ninth inning. There is a man on third. The ball is hit. The man on third base runs, slides into home base just a fraction of a second before the ball snaps in the catcher's mit. The umpire throws up his arms and shouts, "Safe!" It is in this same spirit of excitement and game-winning that Paul begins the eighth chapter of Romans. Paul shouts, "Safe!" "There is *no* condemnation *now* for those who are in Jesus Christ!" (8:1) No person, no cause, no law can condemn us. We are free! We are as safe as if we were already in heaven. For Paul this statement of safety needs no argument or proof. God as the umpire of life has made the decision; we are safe at home! The game is won!

Paul then proceeds to tell us how we are safe and winners in Christ Jesus. It is because of "the law of the Spirit" which has won out over "the law of sin and death" (8:2). The law of the Spirit accomplishes what the law of sin and death have failed to do — that the will of God might be fulfilled.

Law

The use of the word "law" here is very confusing. Paul does not use it in the usual sense of a rule or regulation; rather he uses it to denote *authority*. Sin has no more authority over us. Now, according to Paul, the Spirit has authority over us. We are freed, liberated, emancipated. The verb used here is in the aorist tense which denotes, "once for all." Our freedom in Christ is forever. It is for eternity!

Free to Be Me

How can Paul say that we are free and at the same time say that we are under absolute authority of the Spirit? This is possible because the Spirit enables us to be what we were intended to be. I am free to be me — the "me" God intended me to be!

All of us want to be accepted and loved. We want to be whole persons, not estranged from God and ourselves. Before Christ, when we were under the power of sin and death, we were not our own true selves. Without God we were lost and alone. We were like sheep without a shepherd. We were prodigals starving in a foreign land among strangers. Christ seeks and finds us, brings us home, and gives to us the Spirit of God that enables us to be accepted as God's children and find harmony within ourselves, self-acceptance, and wholeness.

A fish cannot live without water. Therefore, we could say that the fish lives under the authority of water. He must be in the water, surrounded by it in order to live. So Paul views the authority of the Spirit over us; we must be in the Spirit and under the authority of the Spirit if we are to live. In other words, Paul is saying we are in our natural habitat, we are at home only when we are in the Spirit and the Spirit is in us. Christ brings us home — brings us home safe!

Flesh and Spirit

All through the eighth chapter of Romans two words are repeated again and again. These two words are flesh (*sarx*) and Spirit (*pneuma*). It is important that we understand what Paul means when he uses these two words.

Flesh. In his writings Paul uses the word "flesh" in several different ways. Sometimes he uses the word "flesh" in the narrow sense, the literal sense of the physical flesh of the body. At other times Paul uses the word "flesh" in the broader sense as "looking at things from the human point of view." But here in the eighth chapter of Romans Paul uses the term "flesh" in the broadest sense of the word. Here it means the totality of human nature apart from God. Flesh means everything that separates us from God and attaches us to the world. It also means to live a life dominated by self rather than God.

We must not, however, equate flesh exclusively with the physical body and worldly actions such as sex crimes and murder. Paul includes in the sins of the flesh such non-material expressions of our personhood as idolatry, hatred, greed, strife, jealousy, and envy. The sins of the flesh involve our minds and wills as well as our physical bodies. Flesh is all that we are, all that we think and feel and do apart from God.

Spirit. The Spirit is the Spirit of God which comes to us as a power and works within us, uniting us with God and thereby enabling us to willingly obey God's will in our life. Spirit is the exact opposite of flesh. As flesh means what we are and do apart from God, Spirit is what we are and do when we are in God's power.

Two Kinds of Life

In Romans chapter eight, Paul draws this contrast by referring to two kinds of life or ways of living — living according to the flesh or according to the Spirit. The life of the flesh has one focus and center — self; it is a life lived to satisfy one's own desires. The life of the Spirit is to live with God as the focus and center; it is a life lived to please God and God alone.

Paul sees these two lives as going in diametrically different directions. This must *not* be viewed as standing at a fork in the road with two ways of life laid out before us. We are not on neutral ground confronted by a choice as to which way to go. Paul is speaking to Christians, and therefore, those who are already on the right road and going in the right direction. Paul says, "But you are not in the flesh, you are in the Spirit." The issue is not our choice but our response to the fact that we have been chosen. The Spirit of God has chosen us. Therefore, the situation is like being placed in the strong current of a river that is flowing in the direction of God. We can relax and permit the Spirit to carry us to an obedient life before God, or we can exercise the power of the flesh in us and decide to swim up stream, against the current of the Spirit, and thereby swim away from God. Paul encourages us to continue in the way we have been given. He appeals to us to move forward in the life of the Spirit.

Saint and Sinner

One of the most difficult things Paul has to say to us is that in this world we are at the same time both saint and sinner. To begin an understanding of this concept we need to look at a person as Paul does.

Paul takes the biblical view of a person and sees each person as a unity. This is not our way of thinking. We view the human personality as a composite of parts. We commonly speak of body and mind, or body and soul, or the material and the spiritual. This dualism comes from Greek philosophy and is in direct contrast to the thought patterns of the Bible.

The Greeks believed the spiritual soul was caged in the physical body. The soul was good, the body evil. When this idea was adopted into Christian thought, it historically led to all kinds of abuses of the body. The physical body was despised and neglected. People, thinking that they were pleasing God, denied and tortured their bodies. Death was welcomed as the time when the soul would be released from the prison of the body and would fly upward to its home in heaven.

Not Soul but Life

One of the reasons why this Greek way of thinking about a person as body and soul established such a strong foothold in Christian thought is the unfortunate translation of Genesis 2:7, where it says: "And the Lord God formed man of the dust of the ground and breathed into his nostrils the breath of life; and man became a living soul" (KJV). The word in Hebrew which is translated "soul" is *nephesh*, which simply means "life." It is not something distinct and different from the physical body but a characteristic of the total body. We are living bodies — living persons. What the Bible is saying here is that we are given *life* by God our Creator. No dualism of body and soul is meant.

Dualism of Relationship

The Scriptures in general and Paul in particular do, however, speak of a dualism, not a dualism of body and soul, mind and matter, physical and spiritual, but a dualism based on our total relationship to God. One side of this dualism is designated the "old man," "being in Adam," "of the flesh," "living under sin and death." This is the wrong relationship with God.

The other side of this dualism is designated as "the new man," "being in Christ," "in the Spirit." This is the right relationship to God. This is righteousness.

This, for Paul, is the dualism of human personality — not two separate entities or parts which fit together to form a person or a personality, but two basic opposing forces, powers that create two different relationships that can exist between God and us.

According to the Scriptures, we are a psychophysical unit. Mind and matter are blended into a single personality. As God is one, so are we. God can, therefore, address us in an I-Thou relationship. When God speaks to us he addresses our total self, not some special or holy aspect of our personality. Because of Adam and the presence of sin in our world, we are born under the authority of the flesh. We are in a wrong relationship with God — not part of us but all of us. The way of the flesh rules over us. So when God speaks to us, either we do not hear him, or hearing him, we refuse to really listen and do what he commands.

When we believe in Christ, according to Paul, we are given the Spirit of God. As we noted at the beginning of this discussion, the game is won — but, adds Paul, the game is not over. When the Spirit of God, which assures for us the winning of the game, enters us, our lives become a battleground where flesh and Spirit struggle to exercise rule over us. This is the dualism of which Paul speaks — the battle of the flesh and the Spirit both contending for the totality of our being. The flesh does not take our lower nature and the Spirit our higher nature. No! Both Spirit and flesh desire our total self. We are, therefore, saint and sinner at the same time. We are sinner as the flesh directs us; we are saint as the Spirit directs us.

This battle within us continues until death when the Spirit wins, and the power the flesh has over us is destroyed. This is assured because of the death and Resurrection of our Lord and Savior. The battle within us he fought on Calvary and has, therefore, assured for us the victory.

A New Body

We must not, however, make the mistake of equating the flesh with the body. The power of the flesh is destroyed at our death, but our bodies are not cast aside like so much trash. Rather, our bodies are now under the exclusive rule of the Spirit and are thereby transformed as glorified bodies and inherit eternal life as we receive this life — as a total person.

Victory

In the eighth chapter of Romans Paul speaks of our minds set on the "things of the flesh," or, in contrast, set on "the things of the Spirit." Thus, he presents the dualism discussed above. But he does not stop here with a description of the battle which rages within us between flesh and Spirit, he adds the positive note of victory. Paul says, "But you are not in the flesh, you are in the Spirit" (8:9). This is Paul's way of presenting the victory of the Spirit over the flesh; we are victors as we are in the Spirit. We are victorious saints and sinners. As a sinner our victory is assured by God's continuous forgiveness. As a saint our victory is that we are one with our God.

The day will come when saint will win out over sinner, but before that time much blood, sweat and tears will be shed. The battle will go on daily. The important thing is that we are not to lose heart. The battle in us will be won. We have God's good word on that!

Death and Life

Our destiny depends on the direction our life takes. When we go the way of the Spirit, we move in the direction of ultimately winning the game. When we oppose the Spirit and go our way of the flesh, we are losing the game. In the game of football, for example, there are times when we move in the right direction, gaining yardage toward a touchdown. There are other times when we lose yardage and go in the wrong direction. So the Christian experience is a daily dying and rising again.

Some are inclined to ask, "But is it not true that in the end we lose no matter how we play the game, for we will all die?" Paul's answer is that such a question reflects a shortsighted view of the end of this game of life. True, all of us will die because we are involved in the human situation which is under the condemnation of death. Sin came into the world and with sin came death. But Paul adds, "if Christ lives in you, the Spirit is life, for you have been put right with God even though your bodies are going to die because of sin" (8:10 TEV).

Then follows verse eleven (not included in our lesson) which further clarifies the matter: "If the Spirit of God, who raised Jesus from death, lives in you, then he who raised Christ from death will also give life to your mortal bodies by the presence of his Spirit in you" (TEV). We die but we die with Christ and therefore rise with him. We who are in Christ share in the victory of the Resurrection. We who are in the Spirit are moving in the direction of life; physical death is but an inevitable interlude that has to be passed through on the way. For those who walk in the life of the flesh, death is the final end; but for us who walk in the Spirit, death is only an experience encountered on the way to unending life.

In 1942 Boston College had a great football team. They defeated every opponent by an average of 26 points. That is, until the closing game of the season against Holy Cross. Before the game the sports writers called it a "mismatch" because the Holy Cross Crusaders had been able to win only four of the nine games they had played that year.

To everyone's surprise an upset happened that Saturday afternoon. Everything went wrong for Boston College. On the other hand the Crusaders could do no wrong. Final score: Holy Cross 55 — Boston College 12.

The Boston team was crushed and crawled back to the campus.

Most of the team went to bed stunned and disappointed. The big victory party planned at the Coconut Grove Night Club was cancelled.

The next morning the players woke, cringing at the thought of facing the headlines in the papers about the big upset and defeat. But the outcome of the game was overshadowed by the headlines that the Coconut Grove Night Club had burned and more than four hundred people had lost their lives in the holocaust. Their defeat in football had saved them from a fiery death.

When we look at the experience of death at the end of our life, it can look like a defeat. The final score is against us and we lose the game. It is life's final disappointment and defeat. We have lost. It is all over. We go to sleep stunned with sorrow. Then morning comes, we awake, and suddenly discover that our death is not the end. Our death as been but a step in the process of our salvation. We are real winners, for in death God gives us life — new life in a world that has no end.

In our study of this text we are back at the beginning with Paul, shouting, "There is no condemnation for those who are in Christ!" And now we can add our voice to his and shout, "And no death either! No final death! Thanks be to God!" We are safe at home plate! In Christ we are all winners! Thanks be to God!

We Are All Adopted

Fifth Sunday in Lent

Romans 8:11-19

During a colloquium at Princeton Theological Seminary, the professor posed a simple question to the seminar of budding theologians, "Who is a Christian?"

The answers given by the students in the discussion which followed were not simple but reflected the spectrum of current fads in religious thinking. Each seemed to ride his own theological hobbyhorse. One quoted Bonhoeffer and said, "A Christian is a man for others." Another, reflecting Tillich, said, "A Christian is one with ultimate concern." Some pointed to Baptism as the mark of the Christian. Others mentioned being a member of the church. Still others would stress the importance of creeds and formulas of belief. Many stressed social awareness, saying, "A Christian is one who challenges the sick social order." Those with a pentecostal experience mentioned, "born again," "gifts of healing." One even insisted on the "gift of tongues" as the acid test of being a Christian.

Finally one student spoke up, "These definitions are all activist, focusing on what a Christian does, not what he or she *is*! I want to know if your man or woman is a Christian when they are asleep?"

That gets to the heart of the matter. What is it that establishes persons as Christians when they are asleep — when they are doing nothing but simply being themselves? To be a Christian refers to what we are — our status, our nature, our inner being, our identity as a person. True, what we are is reflected in what we do, but the question is not, "What does a Christian do?" but "Who is a Christian?"

In Romans 8:11-19 Paul gives his answer to this question. He says that a Christian is one who has been adopted into the family of God and thereby becomes a son or daughter of God. And, we might add, we are children of God when we are asleep, as well as when we are awake and active.

Adoption

This metaphor of adoption which Paul uses to describe a Christian has many implications for Paul, so it is important that at the beginning of our discussion we examine carefully the term "adoption."

The people to whom Paul was writing this letter lived in Rome, and Roman practices of adoption were serious actions. Much of the seriousness of adoption was based on the social fact that the father had absolute power over his family. He literally owned every member of the family and had over them the power of life or death.

Consequences

The consequences of adoption made it a serious step in Roman culture. According to Barclay there were four main consequences.

1. The adopted person lost all legal rights in his old family and gained all rights in the new family. He was literally dead to his old life and began a new life with adoption.

2. The adopted child became heir to his new father's estate. Even if blood-sons were born after the adoption, it did not affect his rights. To assure this, the adoption ceremony was carried on in the presence of seven witnesses. This extreme caution would assure the adopted son of his inheritance when the foster father died. In any dispute about the rights of the adopted son to inherit, one or more of the witnesses was legally required to step forward voluntarily and swear the adoption to be genuine.

3. By law, all debts incurred before adoption were cancelled, completely free even of moral obligation. The adopted child was considered a new person entering into a completely new life.

4. In the eyes of society and the law, the adopted child was of the "blood" of the family. For example, if an adopted boy fell in love with the daughter of his new father, he could not marry her because they were of the same blood and it would be an act of incest.

As we read Romans 8:11-19, we can see these consequences reflected in what Paul says about our adoption into the family of God. As adopted children of God our past debts are cancelled (8:12). We come under the complete control of God (8:14). We literally have a new father (8:15). We are heirs of the father and have his inheritance (8:17), and our inheritance is assured by witnesses (8:16).

Paul uses the metaphor of adoption to proclaim that in Jesus Christ God adopts the debt-laden, poverty-stricken fatherless sinners, and they become by his grace debt-free inheritors of the Kingdom.

Carroll O'Conner, better known as Archie Bunker, has an adopted son. On a talk show he was asked how he told his son about the adoption. O'Conner's answer is classic. He said: "When the boy was old enough to understand, I sat him down and told him, 'Many years ago your mother and I met each other. We loved each other and adopted each other. Later we met you, fell in love with you and adopted you. That means that everybody in this family is adopted.' "

This is what Paul is saying to us. In the kingdom of God everybody is adopted.

The Deeds of the Body

Paul then proceeds to present the implications of our adoption as children of God. He says we are to "put to death the deeds of the body" (8:13). He does not say we are to deny the body or kill it. He does not call us to a suicide of the flesh. Rather, he says that we are to destroy the *deeds* of the body. The body is purified, but not by beating it into submission. The purity of the body will come about through submission in the Spirit. We are not to torture ourselves but permit the transformation of our body which this new status of adoption will bring about.

Our body which was once a den of evil will now become the temple of God. Our new relationship to our body is well expressed in chapter twelve of Romans where Paul states: "We present our body as a living sacrifice, holy and acceptable unto the Lord."

Led by the Spirit

As we are not to beat our bodies into submission so we are not to be driven by the Spirit. Paul says: For all who are *led* by the Spirit of God are sons of God" (8:14). By this Paul means we are not beaten and driven by a whip like slaves forcing us in fear to become obedient children; rather we are gently led by the Spirit.

Musicians who had the privilege of playing under the great conductor Toscanini have said, "He brought out from me musical skills I never knew I possessed." So the Spirit directs our lives, bringing out a goodness we never knew we possessed. In fact we did not possess it until we became the adopted children of God. But now possessing it we need the Spirit to bring it forth. This the Spirit does, not driving us but drawing from us the goodness we have been given.

And it follows that the beautiful, harmonious music our lives produce is not the source which causes or brings about our salvation; our new way of living is outward evidence that we are new persons under the direction of the Spirit of God.

Leonard Bernstein, conductor-composer, has said of his composing, "If summer does not sing within you then nothing sings within you; and unless something sings within you, you cannot make music." So Paul says the Spirit sings within us and because of this we can make great music.

Not Slaves but Sons

In support of the leading rather than the driving of the Spirit, Paul adds: "For you did not receive the spirit of slavery to fall back into fear, but you have received the spirit of sonship" (8:15). Our new relationship with God is not that of servitude to a hard task-master, but that of fellowship with a loving father.

Abba

This fellowship with the Father is expressed with tender emotion. Paul reaches back into the language of his own childhood when he writes: "When we cry, 'Abba! Father!, it is the Spirit, himself, bearing witness with our spirit that we are the children of God" (8:15b-16).

The word "Abba," which Jesus used in the address of his Lord's Prayer, and Paul uses here to describe the warm relation that exists between us and God, literally means "Daddy." It expresses the deepest affection, and the most profound sense of kinship between a child and his father.

The word "Abba" has its roots in *baby talk*. Most languages have similar words for children's terms for parents — Mamma - Papa - Dada. The reason for this is simple. They originate in baby talk. Baby is sitting on the floor exercising his vocal cords, making nonsensical sounds. As he does, quite involuntarily a sound comes out, "ma-ma-ma-ma." Suddenly mother rushes over, picks baby up and cuddles him. "You said my name! You called me Mama!" she says. The truth is, he hasn't; baby was just making noises. However, he learns quickly that certain noises bring special responses from adults and instinctively he repeats them when he wants attention.

So in ancient Israel, baby made the sounds of "ab-ba, ab-ba," and a whiskered young Jew exclaimed, "He knows me! My son called my name!"

All of this lies behind Paul's joyous use of the term, "Abba." Paul says in this new relationship with God the Father, there is the same intimacy and warmth of a baby with its doting parents.

For many of us the thought of calling God "Daddy" is disrespectful. It seems to ignore the holy dignity of divinity. We need to remember, however, that when the Pope comes out to greet the crowds in St. Peter's square and stands there in the stately grandeur of his rich robes, on a balcony draped with the great papal coat-of-arms, the response of the people is to cry out, *"Il papa! Il papa!"* This is certainly not an act of disrespect; rather, it is the highest reverence the Catholic people can offer to their supreme spiritual leader.

The Spirit With Our Savior

So often when we talk of the relationship between ourselves and God, we tend to divide up the experience of salvation so that certain actions are attributed to God and others are attributed to us. God acts and we respond. God demands and we obey. This is similar to the stimulus-response pattern of science. Wherever there is an effect, there must be a cause.

This is not the approach Paul takes. He sees God as active in the total process of salvation. God acts toward us and then he acts in us. God demands and then gives us the response of obedience as a gift. Paul puts it this way: "When we cry 'Abba! Father!' it is the Spirit himself bearing witness with our spirit that we are the children of God" (8:15b-16).

The first Spirit is capitalized; the second is not. The first Spirit is God; the second refers to us. Therefore, what Paul is saying is that when we call God "Father," it is God's response in us to himself. Or in other words, we do nothing by our own strength apart from God. Even when we respond to his love offer and call him "Father," it is not us by ourselves calling God "Father" but the Spirit of God in us and through us calling God "Father."

So often in sermons we hear what we *must* do. We must believe, have faith, serve, sacrifice, live good and moral lives. We are called to act in response to God's action. The impression is that of a teeter-totter. God and grace sit on one end, and we with our faith sit on the other end. God exercises his strength and up we go; then we exercise our strength and up goes God! Nothing could be further from the thinking of Paul. We have no weight or strength on our end. If salvation depended in any degree on us, God would be forever "down," and we would always be "up"!

In Paul's thought, God is on both ends of the teeter-totter!

There is a movement from grace to faith; God demands and we are to obey; but our response and obedience is God at work in us — "the Spirit himself bearing witness with our spirit" (8:16).

Joint Heirs

Paul has established our identity as children of God, and then he adds, "and if children then heirs, heirs of God and fellow heirs with Christ" (8:17). As God is our Father, Jesus is our brother, for we are joint heirs with Christ. Joint heirs receive equally. This assures us of the certainty of our inheritance of the kingdom and its salvation. As the Father gives the kingdom to his only begotten Son, Jesus Christ, so by our adoption we share equally in this kingdom.

The full implications of Paul's witness are staggering! What Christ is by nature, we are by grace. We are not only related to God the Father as sons and daughters, but we are given the full status and privilege of being true sons and daughters who inherit the riches of the kingdom. We are the chosen people. We are the people of the promise!

Suffering and Splendor

Suddenly Paul introduces the issue of suffering. He writes: "fellow heirs with Christ, provided we suffer with him" (8:17b). He has been building up an elevated and glowing picture of us as adopted sons and daughters of God, joint heirs with Christ. He has spoken of the promise of our great inheritance as the chosen people, and then suddenly he adds a provision, "provided we suffer with him."

It is clear that Paul is not pausing here to deal with the difficult theological question of why people suffer — the tough issues of babies born blind or crippled, people suffering and dying from cancer, starvation and the innocent slaughtering of war victims; rather, Paul is acting not as a theologian at all, but as a pastor.

Paul is writing to the Christians at Rome, and as he speaks of the glories of being a Christian, he thinks to himself, "I wonder how these people will react to what I am saying? They are living hard and bitter lives. They live in distressing conditions and are plagued with troubles and suffering. Will all this talk of glory sound at best like 'pie in the sky' to them?"

Therefore, in order to help his people reconcile the trials, troubles and tribulations they daily experience with the great and wonderful things he is saying, Paul points to the suffering of

Christ, and says that we share Christ's suffering.

This is a hard saying! It is not any easier to understand it now than it was then. Therefore, three things need to be noted:

1. The translation here is important. Most translations read, "provided we suffer," or "if we suffer." It could, however, also be translated "since we share Christ's suffering." This seems more reasonable, for Paul is not suddenly placing a provision on our blessing of grace — we will receive the glory that is to come *if we suffer*; rather Paul is pointing out that our present suffering is proof that we are with Christ, and since we are with Christ in his sufferings we will also be with him in his glory.

2. Christians did not have to be urged or directed to suffer; they knew suffering as a way of life. Knowing this, Paul refers to their suffering as a mark of Christ upon them, like a brand burned into their very being. This brand, this mark was the sign of assurance that they belonged to Christ and were with him. Because Christ was with them and they were with Christ and they shared this common experience of suffering, their suffering was different. Their suffering was, therefore, but a prelude and the promise of the splendor which was to come. Paul is saying, "I know you suffer, and *you* know you suffer, therefore know with as much certainty that one day you will share Christ's glory."

3. Christ suffered because he was the Son of God; so our suffering is evidence that we are God's sons and daughters.

Often, Christ had pointed out to this disciples that the world knows its own, and since he belonged to God and not to the forces and powers of this world, he is hated by the world. The world persecutes him and causes him to suffer precisely because of his relationship to the Father (John 15:18). The world is under the control of evil; hence the world hates God, his Son and us.

God not the Author of Suffering

The important thing is that we do not come to the conclusion that God is the author of suffering, that he causes us to suffer in order to prepare us and make us worthy of the splendor which is to come.

A teacher in high school stood his ground on the issue that sex education should be a part of the school curriculum. Several families stood by him. The community was incensed by the very idea. Tempers flared. The situation got out of hand. The families that stood by the teacher were harrassed and tormented They received nasty phone calls, had rocks thrown through their windows and had their tires slashed.

It was not the teacher who did this to those who stood by him. No! But the fact that they stood on his side meant they stood against the feelings of the community and suffered the abuse that was aimed at him.

So Paul says of us. God is not the author of our sufferings; the world is! As we stand with God, we are hated as he is hated by the world, and we suffer the abuses the world aims at him.

The Name-Tag of Christ

Paul does not end on this note of suffering but adds: "we suffer with him in order that we may also be glorified with him." In this season of Lent, as we look at the cross, we see not just a pathetic figure dying in agony; we see the King of Glory establishing the rule of God in our world. This figure on the cross is not victim, but victor. And because his cross is our cross, we are united in this act and become through his blood true sons and daughters of God.

During World War I two young men were in a muddy trench somewhere on the battlefields of Normandy. One young man was wounded and dying. His buddy held him in his arms and cried out into the darkness, "It ain't right! I'm a poor nobody with nothing to live for. My buddy is rich with everything to live for — yet he's the one that's dying. It ain't right! Oh, God, it ain't right!"

Hearing this, the dying young man reached up and tore the identification tag from his own neck and handed it to his buddy. "Here take this," he said, "and I'll take yours. In the morning when they find me, your old life will be dead and you can begin a new life with my name."

"I can't," his friend mumbled through his tears. "You must!" the dying soldier came back. "Let me live in you." And with that he pressed the identification tag, cutting, into his friend's hand with the grip of death, and died.

This is what happened on Calvary. Suffering on the cross, dying for us, our Lord took the identification tag of his sonship and with his nail-pierced, bloody hands, pressed it into our hands with a grip that can never be broken!

So we bear Christ's name! But more, we bear his very life in us — his inheritance as God's own son. By his suffering and death, by his body and blood, we are sealed as adopted sons and daughters of God!

God Glorified

Sunday of the Passion

Philippians 2:5-11

This Sunday is the first day of Holy Week. Originally it was called Passion Sunday. Because the day usually began with a procession of palms it was nicknamed "Palm Sunday." In the Three Year Lectionary the historic name of the day is restored, Sunday of the Passion, and only subtitled, Palm Sunday. On this day two dominant themes are presented — humiliation and exaltation.

The Jewish hope was that one day a Messiah would come from the House of David. Like David he would be a great king and lift the Jews to an exalted position over all other nations.

Jesus came as the Messiah, but not the one the Jews expected. He came not as a king but as a servant. He entered Jerusalem as a humble, meek, lowly, servant-king, mounted not on a royal thoroughbred but on a common beast of burden. In their excitement the Jewish people ignored the symbol of his lowly transportation. They wanted a hero, noble and royal, so they exalted this gentle Jew, this common son of a carpenter, this rusty peasant, this donkey-rider, and treated him as if he were their long-awaited king. These Messiah-makers threw their clothing before him, waved branches of palms and shouted, "Hosanna to the Son of David."

The witness of the historic Church agreed with this enthusiastic response of the crowd and labeled this event as the "Triumphant Entrance into Jerusalem."

When Jesus embarked upon his ministry, he considered the royal role of Davidic Messiahship, but he chose instead the messiahship depicted in the great Servant Poem of the Old Testament, Isaiah 53, where glorification and kingly coronation are accomplished and acclaimed in suffering servanthood. The Second Lesson for this day, Philippians 2:5-11, reflects the language and thought of this ancient Servant Poem and forms the theological basis for a Sunday of the Passion.

Love Letter

In the truest sense Paul's letter to the church at Philippi was a love letter from a spiritual father to his children in the faith. The people at Philippi were Paul's favorite congregation, one to which he turned with evident satisfaction as a pastor, and from which he received, at various times, generous offerings for the support of his missionary adventures.

Philippi was a city in Macedonia and marks the beginning of the movement of the gospel to us here in the West, for this is where Paul first set foot in Europe. He had come because of a voice and vision which called him to "come over into Macedonia and help us" (Acts 16:9).

The absence from the Philippian church of heresies and major controversies of doctrine which plagued other Christian communities gave Paul the opportunity to speak in the Philippian letter of the great foundations on which all personal faith is established — unity with Christ. This "being in Christ" is the source and substance of the Christian style of life.

Philippians 2:5-11, however, seems to indicate that even in this model congregation, some elements of strife were manifesting themselves and threatening the peace and harmony of the congregation. It seems that in a shuffle for leadership there was evidence of self-seeking and rivalry. Paul was determined to nip this self-seeking in the bud before it did any damage to the congregation that had been the source of so much joy for him. So Paul directs his people's attention to the danger of self-interest which can so easily enter into and dominate all of us because of our natural heritage from the world.

Self-Preservation

The undeniable link we have with our animal brethren of this world is the instinct for self-preservation. At the center of our lives, self sits enthroned. If any challenge comes to its authority, immediately every emergency attribute we possess comes to life, takes off its coat, rolls up its sleeves and is ready for protective and aggressive action.

In many ways this is good. For without this instinct for preservation, our bodies would not fight off disease; if we were not given food, we would starve. There would be no motivation to persevere against adversities. In an antagonistic world we would recoil to a cowardly retreat and hide in caves of fear and indifference and soon die.

On the other hand concern for self is the basis of many evils that disturb and disrupt life. Particularly, the social and personal difficulties that plague us are traceable in part to self-centeredness, self-love, and self-pity. Family life is destroyed when various members of the household place self-interest ahead of the welfare of the family. Our current inflation is to a large extent the result of the struggle of management and labor to achieve self-benefits at the expense of sound economy. Competition without controls leads to corruption and exploitation and everyone suffers. Patriotism degenerates into narrow-minded nationalism and drives countries to wage wars of aggression and colonialism. All areas of our modern political and economic life are saturated with the greed for self-advancement.

The Mind of Christ

The tragedy is that from this trap of self we cannot free ourselves. In his letter to the Philippians, Paul gives a way out of the snare of self-centeredness. He writes: "Have this mind among yourselves, which is yours in Jesus Christ" (2:5). The mind of Christ! As we are in him and he is in us, we possess an exit, an escape from the imprisonment of self. Mind here means more than the brain, or the intellect; it means the total person. To possess the mind of Christ means to be possessed totally by Christ.

Picture Portrait

Paul then looks at the total Christ and presents a picture portrait of the passion of our Lord.

First, Paul says, "though he (Christ) was in the form of God, he did not count equality with God a thing to be grasped" (2:6). Paul is very careful in his choice of words here. There are two words in the Greek language that are translated into the English word "form." There is the word *morphe* which refers to the essential form of something, a form which never changes. In spite of all circumstances it remains the same.

The other Greek word translated into the English word "form" is *schema* which refers to outward form. This form changes from time to time according to circumstances.

When these two Greek words are used to describe a person, *morphe* would refer to the unchangeable quality of a person such as male or female. *Schema* would be used when describing the outward or physical appearances which do change in the process of growth — from baby, to child, to youth, to middle age, to old age.

As a person grows older, the hair turns white, the skin wrinkles, the "middle" expands and, in general, energy declines. This is *schema*.

When Paul speaks of Jesus being in the form of God, he uses the word *morphe*, the form that never changes. This is Paul's way of making it crystal clear that Jesus was essentially, unalterably, and unchangeably God. Jesus did not just come from God; he was God.

Having established his belief in the divinity of Christ, Paul then proceeds to point out that Jesus did not consider his divinity "a thing to be grasped." This means that Jesus did not hug divinity to himself jealously or possessively like a child would cling to his security blanket, refusing to let it go. Jesus did not exploit his divine nature. He did not flaunt it, or revel in it for his own glorification; "but emptied himself taking the form of a servant, being born in the likeness of men" (2:7).

The reference here is clearly to the Incarnation. The divine Christ was born a human baby, accepting all the limitations that such an action incurred. He was born helpless, depending upon human parents to feed and clothe him, care for and nurture him. For thirty years he was a carpenter's son, knowing the sweat of toil, tired and aching muscles, the pain of physical injury, mental anguish, sorrow and disappointment. At the same time he knew the refreshment of a cool drink of water, the pleasure of laughter with good friends, the satisfying enjoyment of tasty food, the warmth of kindness and love.

Emptied Himself

When Jesus Christ was born in "the likeness of men," did this mean that Christ put aside his divinity and left it in heaven when he came to earth? At first reading it would seem that Paul is implying this when he uses the phrase "emptied himself." The word "emptied" is seldom used when talking about a person. We empty the contents of a container, a bottle, a jug, or a box, but here Paul says that Christ "emptied himself." Does this mean that Christ emptied himself of his divinity and was therefore no longer divine?

Here the Greek language is helpful, for the Greek word that is translated "taking" is an aorist active participle, and in the Greek language defines the action of the main verb of the sentence. The part of the sentence that concerns us is, "but emptied himself, taking the form of a servant, being born in the likeness of men." The main verb is "emptied." The participial phrase is "*taking* the form of a servant." Since the participial phrase defines the main verb, this would mean that Paul is not saying that Jesus emptied himself of his divine nature but he "emptied himself" by becoming a servant. Being divine Christ took upon himself the nature of the Suffering Servant. As the divine Son of God, Jesus Christ would serve and suffer for our sakes.

Paul used the strong word "emptied" because he did not want anyone to get the idea that Jesus was simply playing a role of servant. This was no playacting. This was the real thing. The Son of God became *the* servant.

Frequently, stories are told of kings who dress in pauper's rags and walk the streets of their kingdom to see and experience how people live. The action of Christ was not like this. He did not accept the outward appearances of a servant or simply act like a servant; Christ became the Servant-God.

Remembering that Paul's main concern in this letter is pastoral, we must not read what he is saying as if he were developing a theological doctrine of the two natures of Christ; rather Paul is simply describing what Christ did for us — Christ became a servant. Because of this, we who are to have the "mind among yourselves which is ours in Christ" are also to be servants.

A young executive finally realized his dream. He was the proud owner of a Rolls-Royce. For weeks that is all he could talk about. One day at the club, after a round of golf, he met a man in the locker room who needed a ride into town. Delighted with the opportunity to show off his new Rolls he offered the stranger a lift. As they drove into town he casually asked, "Have you ever ridden in a Rolls before?"

"Well," replied the passenger dryly, "never in the front seat." Quite a put-down!

God gives us a Rolls-Royce life. When he does, however, he puts us in the front seat. What we need to be reminded of again and again is that this is the position of servanthood. We are called to be a chauffeur, driving where God wants us to go. Possessing the "mind of Christ," our lives are moved in the direction God designates. God is the master of our lives; we go where he wants. No longer does self give the orders, but obeys them.

The Cross

Jesus was the obedient servant to such a degree that he was ready not only to die but to accept death in its most ignominious and painful form, death on a cross. In agony, in public shame, he hung naked, without relief, without dignity. He accepted the full and total power of death, for only then could he accomplish the full and total triumph of life over death.

Victor, Not Victim

This is what makes the dying Christ victor and not victim. "Therefore," (because of this) writes Paul, "God has highly exalted him and bestowed on him the name which is above every name, that at the name of Jesus every knee should bow, in heaven and on earth, and under the earth and every tongue confess that Jesus Christ is Lord" (2:9-11). The name of "Jesus" means *savior*. The phrase "Jesus is Lord" was the first confession of the early church. And by this confession they witnessed to the world that he was Lord of the universe, Lord over all that existed.

Christ rendered perfect obedience to the Father, and it did not go unrecognized. He was rewarded. He was resurrected. God raised him from the dead. Note. Christ did not rise from the grave by his own power; the resurrected life was a gift. God the Father raised Christ Jesus from the dead. The importance of this distinction is that in Christ we, who are helpless and have no power of our own, share this Resurrection, for it is a gift; as Christ, the servant of God, was raised from the grave, so shall we as servants be raised from the dead.

His Glory

There have been many stories told of people who through courage, risk and the willingness to make a sacrifice have risen from rags to riches; but never was there a story to match this. Jesus willingly submitted himself to the status of servant. He bowed to all the reproach and infamy of a world polluted by sin; he is raised to a position of such homage that the whole universe falls to its knees before the glory and splendor of Lord Jesus. Before this accolade, the cheers of his Jerusalem entrance fade into oblivion. The true triumph of our Christ is not that the people hailed him as King, but that God declared him to be Lord.

Our Glory

As the Father glorified Jesus, so also will he glorify us. Not as we imitate Christ but as we are in Christ and possess the mind of Christ. Our self-humiliation, even our efforts at willing obedience, are not the source of our glorification. Unlike Christ we merit no reward. By our own strength we can not humble ourselves and practice perfect obedience. This is why these words of Paul are such good news to us. He does not say "Be like Christ; do what he did. Empty yourself and become servants, be obedient unto death even the death of a cross." No. Rather Paul declares, "have this mind among yourselves, *which is yours* in Christ Jesus " (2:5). We are not to achieve through self-effort the mind of Christ; it is already ours, "which is yours" says Paul. We are to partake, participate, share in, realize and utilize what has been given to us as a gift in Christ.

This means that we will first suffer with Christ, if we are to be glorified with him. We will die with him, if we are to be raised with him. But after all, we will suffer and die anyway even without being in him. We have no choice. Suffering and death are our lot, our fate. But in Christ our futile fate is transformed into a divine destiny. In Christ we become like him, not victims of suffering and death but victors. This is our divine destiny which belongs to those who are in Christ.

Glory of God

Through humiliation to glorification, through suffering to salvation, through death to life — this is the path Paul points out to us. But then he adds the gleaming goal to which this path points, "to the glory of God the Father" (2:11) — from death to life for the glory of God the Father. The ultimate end of our humiliation and exaltation is the glory of God our Creator.

Jesus does not displace God the Father. He is the means by which we return to our heavenly Father as beloved children. The life, death and Resurrection of Jesus are the work of God. God is not dethroned. Jesus sits at the right hand of the Father. The confession, "Jesus is Lord," resounds to the glory of God the Father.

This is important in the season of Lent when we give special emphasis and attention to the cross-event fulfilling the truth, "If I be lifted up, I will draw all men unto myself." Jesus draws all of us to him that he might carry us before the throne of God the Father and present us worthy to be God's children.

Always we face the danger of "Jesuology," focusing our love and faith so exclusively on Jesus that he becomes the end rather than the means of coming to the Father. Jesus becomes for us the good God; the Father remains the austere, forboding judge of the heavens, rendering verdicts of rewards and punishments based alone on holy justice.

So often we think of God the Father as a stern old man with a white beard and penetrating eyes, pursuing us as we attempt to escape him and participate in secret worldly pleasures. This is reflected in the fact that in all my ministry of dealing with people faced with tragedies and disappointments, I never once heard anyone say, "Why did Jesus let this happen to me?" It is always, "Why did God let this happen?" The Father is the "heavy" in our theological thinking. Jesus is the good guy, our big brother who holds the threatening hand of the Father from us.

How Jesus must weep again and again as we live in our Jerusalems of misunderstanding, failing to know God as a kindly Father of mercy, forgiveness, grace and love. Our Lord came not to serve as a buffer between us and our Father God. Jesus came not to save us from the Father, but from sin, death and the Devil. Jesus came to eliminate all those things that separate us from God and to build a bridge between ourselves and our Creator. Jesus came to open up the heart of God the Father, revealing the warm, compassionate heart of a forgiving and loving Father.

All that our Lord was and did, he was and did to the glory of God the Father. Therefore, as this season of Lent draws to the climax of the cross of death and the open tomb of new life, let us constantly remind ourselves — all this — the cross, the tomb, humiliation, exaltation, all this is the way, the means by which God the Father hugs us and all creation unto himself. All this, therefore, is to the glory of God the Father.

On this Palm Sunday of Passion Christ calls us to spread our garments before the feet of the Father; to wave palm branches honoring the Father; to shout out in joy, "Glory be to God the Father. Amen!"